Czecho-Slovakia Within

Czecho-Slovakia Within

Bertram de Colonna

8 paws ⚜
an army

The Scriptorium

First published in 1938: Bertram de Colonna, *Czecho-Slovakia Within,* Thornton Butterworth, London.

Reprint ©2022 by The Scriptorium.
wintersonnenwende.com
versandbuchhandelscriptorium.com

Notes to our Readers:
#1 - please pardon the occasional wrong hyphenation at the end of lines. The software with which this book is printed inserts these hyphens automatically, and manual corrections of errors are almost impossible.
#2 - in the original 1938 edition of this book, chapters are only numbered, without chapter titles. We (Scriptorium) have added representative chapter titles in this reprint to make the Table of Contents more helpful.

Our cover design is based on the flag of Czechoslovakia adopted in 1920, and on an outline map of Europe, 1929-1938, courtesy of Wikipedia.

Print edition ISBN 978-1-7781445-2-3
ebook ISBN 978-1-7781445-3-0

CONTENTS ▊

CONTENTS

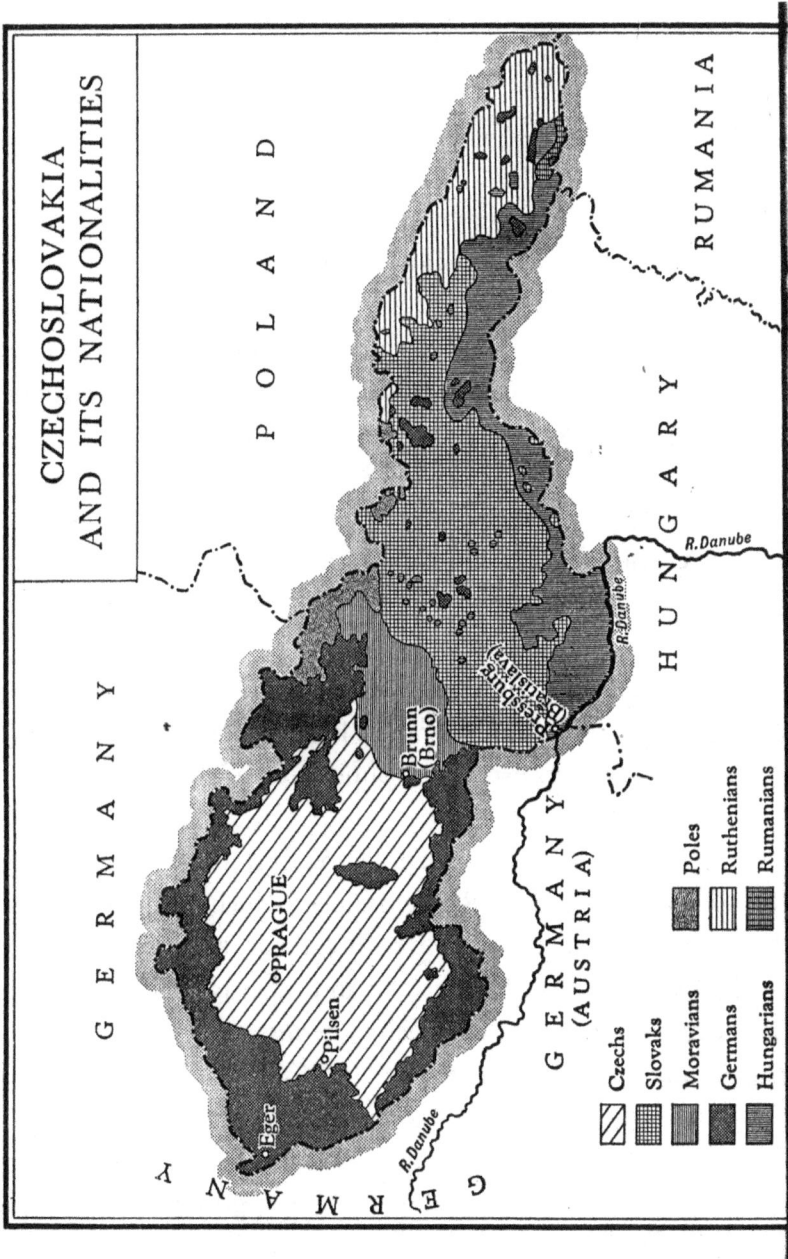

Czechoslovakia and Its Nationalities
Frontispiece from the original 1938 edition.

Introduction

Czecho-Slovakia is a State in the centre of Europe whose existence dates from the Versailles Treaty. It is a country without a coast line, and possessing no rivers from source to mouth; its largest river, the Moldau, is a tributary of the Elbe. If we are to go by the *Handbook of Central and Eastern Europe* Czecho-Slovakia's chief port is Hamburg! The Moldau belongs geographically to the Elbe system.

Czecho-Slovakia's lack of coast line makes the country comparable with Switzerland, though the compactness which characterizes the latter country is lacking.

On the one hand, the State is bounded by the Carpathians and Poland: on the Hungarian frontier there is no natural barrier; the border line cuts through an area extensively populated by Hungarians.

Czecho-Slovakia comprises the provinces of Bohemia, Moravia, Silesia, Slovakia and Carpathian Ruthenia, all of which formerly belonged to the old Austro-Hungarian Empire. It consists, in fact, largely of the remnants of the old Dual Monarchy and inherits problems implicit in the merger of a number of widely differing peoples into one State marked by an ethnographic Babel.

Every accusation brought by England against the Austrian Monarchy in pre-War days is applicable to an even greater degree against present-day Czecho-Slovakia. In the old days there was at least the personal touch, such as our own country knows, and the Kaiser Franz Josef had a wide popularity. To-day the only symbol of unity is the artificial constitution promulgated after the cessation of hostilities. There are no traditions to hold the various parts of this politician-made State together.

Czecho-Slovakia is not an economic entity. Her main river belongs to the German Elbe river system; her border provinces belong, both geographically and economically, to other systems. A glance at the map shows the artificial geographical nature of the State. Its frontiers have no historical or geographical justification and are the results of arbitrary demarcation.

Early History

Czech historians base their country's right of existence upon the belief that Bohemia has from time immemorial been a Czech province. According to them it was annexed by the Hapsburg dynasty at the end of the Middle Ages. Its historic frontiers they aver enclosed a far larger area than do those of the present day.

The peace of Europe has been threatened during the last few months by the fact of the Czecho-Slovakian question. The real crux of the matter is not the land hunger of any bordering State, but is in reality the unnatural formation of the country; in addition the Czechs have failed to carry out those conditions of the Peace Treaty which alone permitted of the creation of their national state.

For the last hundred years Czech historians have endeavoured to make the world believe that Bohemia is of a comparatively recent creation as a German province; even the most cursory glance at European history proves this to be a fact. The whole civilization and culture of the country can be traced to German sources.

The first mention of Bohemia in history shows that it was then populated by a Teutonic tribe, the Marcomanni. This tribe occupied a compact area in that part of present-day Czecho-Slovakia known as Bohemia which the Marcomanni called Bojerheim. That was in the fifth century and the greater part of the tribe migrated to Bavaria somewhere about A.D. 535. The similarity between the names Böhmen and Bayern (the German names for Bohemia and Bavaria) indicates the probability of a common root. After the Marcomanni had left the country their place was taken by the Teutonic Langobards and it was only when they too migrated that Slavs invaded Eastern Bohemia and the Prague district. Archaeological discoveries and local tradition are ample proof of the facts given. Their authenticity has never been questioned by English historians.

The Teutons who first reigned in Bohemia left many traces of their occupation in its marches. No people has a better claim to its native soil and to national self-determination than the Germans of Czecho-Slovakia's frontier provinces.

The first known state of a wholly Czech composition came into existence in the eighth century, long after the formation of a Teutonic State on the banks of the Moldau near Prague and in East Bohemia. These new Czech duchies proved to be extremely bad neighbours. Their fondness for pillage and love of strife was so marked in the first years of their existence that Charlemagne was forced to take punitive action against them. In A.D. 807 the Czech Duke of that time became his vassal; from that day until 1806 Bohemia ceased to have a separate existence but was incorporated as a province of the German Empire.

Its existence during those many centuries was no different to that of any other German province; there appears never to have been any need for successive German Emperors to rule it with an iron hand.

The relations between the Dukes of Bohemia and the German Empire originally founded by Charlemagne were on a perfectly normal footing and remained so throughout the whole of the Middle Ages. The Czech population appear to have been fully aware of the advantages conferred by German rule. Law and order were well kept and individual freedom was everywhere respected to the satisfaction of all men. Even the Dukes of the famous Przemysl line ordered themselves as became loyal lieges of the Empire. They took their part in its battles and worthily earned the laurels bestowed upon them on so many occasions. The city of Prague of the twelfth and thirteenth centuries was as German as any other Imperial city of those days.

Ulrich von Eschenbach, Reimar von Zweter and Ulrich von Frei-burg were frequent guests of the Hradchin, a castle in Prague whose architecture could not be more typically Teutonic. There was a King of Bohemia who won for himself a great reputation as a singer of German *Lieder*. German peasants and yeomen tilled the fertile fields of Bohemia and cleared forest lands in their stolid methodical way, an example followed by their Czech neighbours. Germans brought the plough to Bohemia, introduced the vine and were responsible for many other agricultural innovations.

The Czechs took the plough from the Germans and use the German name to this day. A plough in Czecho-Slovakia is a *pluh;* its German name is *Pflug*. The influence of Germany can be traced in many other fields. In the times of the Przemysls and the Emperors of the House of Luxemburg, old Prague was built by German architects whose work was responsible for its present-day interest and beauty. The guides will tell you that the historic pile known as the Veits Cathedral in Prague was designed by a Czech named Petr Parlé; the actual fact is that the architect responsible was one Peter Parler, a Swabian, whose name has been given this non-German intonation by the Czechs.

The Emperor Charles IV and his descendants are claimed to be of Czech origin; as a matter of fact this ruler had no Czech affiliations, nor had he any ambition towards creating an autonomous Czech state. The motive which underlay his building activities in Prague was jealousy of Vienna and a wish to create what he regarded as a fitting background for his imperial state. All this building was in the German manner, for at that time no indigenous style existed; nor was it desired by the Czechs.

2

Recent History

If we are to believe the chroniclers nobody seems to have noticed the need for a Czecho-Slovakian State during the Middle Ages; the area in question seems to have been perfectly happy as an integral part of the German Empire. Even in those far-off days Czech Nationalists existed, of course, who dreamed of an independent future and displayed an ill-founded hatred for all things Teutonic. But they were few and aroused neither interest nor enthusiasm among their countrymen. These are the men who to-day are treated as evidence of a long-felt anti-German sentiment and the desire for Czech national independence throughout the centuries.

It seems certain that the Czech people and their rulers were well content with their existence under the wings of the German eagle throughout the Middle Ages. There is no evidence of any Czech complaint, moreover, during the last century of their incorporation in the Dual Monarchy.

As is usual, dissatisfaction with the existing conditions and a desire for a separate corporate existence was actually started by a group of ambitious politicians. This start coincided with the publication of *Bohemian History* by Franz Palacky, just over a hundred years ago. He exaggerated the importance of the discontented few and appealed to folklore and to what he described as "mediæval Czech poetry." The existence of these verses cannot be questioned, but their authenticity is open to the gravest doubt. In the opinion of most experts these Grueneberg and Koenigshof MSS. are clever forgeries. Yet the standard Czech history is largely founded on their so-called evidence.

In a recent speech at Karlsbad, Henlein demonstrated the mythical nature of Franz Palacky's claim. Henlein's aim was not the termination of an academic quarrel, but rather the ending of propaganda based on an historic fallacy, a fallacy dangerous to the peace of Europe. It is a fallacy which has given rise to Czech ambitions which go much farther than the frontiers demarcated after the Armistice.

Czech Nationalist ambitions were by no means fully satisfied after the loss of the War by the Central Powers. That they expected a larger share of territory to be accorded to them by their friends in London, Paris and Washington is shown by documents produced at the Peace Conference by the memoirs of prominent Czech politicians and by carefully-prepared maps accompanying those documents. It was claimed that there was a great Czech State in Central Europe in mediæval times which was destroyed by the Germans and which the Czechs wished to see restored. Even President Masaryk, founder and first President of Czecho-Slovakia, alleged that successive Kings of Bohemia had "tried to create a mighty state organization by expansion and dynastic policy in the centre of Europe" and that the Czech State under the Luxemburg princes had extended its boundaries to Cracow and Posen and included Hungary, Styria, Lusatia and, last but not least, Brandenburg. It will be seen that Masaryk's claim was modest, for he might well have included Holland, Italy, North and West Germany, all of which belonged in mediæval times to the same Empire as did Bohemia and Brandenburg! His claim, however, would have had to be qualified by the statement that that Empire was ruled not by Bohemian kings but by German emperors.

The World War was welcomed by those Czech firebrands who saw in it the opportunity to persuade numbers of their fellow countrymen to desert to the Allies and thus curry favour with the latter. There is no doubt that the Entente Powers were aware of Czech territorial ambitions, even before the commencement of hostilities. The Russian Ambassador in Vienna received a memorandum outlining the proposed frontiers of the Czech Nationalist State from Dr. Kramarsch, one of the most prominent members of the Czech movement, some time before the War. Bohemia was to receive Lusatia and most of German Silesia under a Czech Tsar whose marches were to run with those of the Father of All the Russias; a Slav Corridor was to run through Hungary as a connexion between Bohemia and the South Slavs.

Rumania, as envisaged by Kramarsch, was to have been even larger than it is to-day; Hungary was to have been denuded of even more territory than she has actually lost; Serbia was to have received Styria, Klagenfurt, Trieste and Pola. South Germany was to be bestowed upon the Hapsburgs, together with Hesse-Nassau, Westphalia and Hanover; they were to keep Vienna and the Austrian Tyrol, while the whole of Schleswig-Holstein was to be given to the Danes and (as an all-important make weight) France's "security" was to be ensured by the fulfilment of her age-long desire; she was to have, at long last, the left bank of the Rhine.

It will thus be seen that Kramarsch's plan gave satisfaction, not only to his own ambition, but also to the Imperialistic longings of his friends. He was not alone in his dreams. Klofatsch, later to be Defence Minister in Czecho-Slovakia, was ready in May, 1914, with a plan for the disruption of the Dual Monarchy based, confessedly, on the strategic consideration. At his request a map was drawn by Hanus Kuffner, a former Czech Imperial officer, showing the frontiers desired by him. Numerous other politicians, among them one Wladimir Sis, contemplated frontiers extending far beyond those of to-day.

All these Nationalist aspirations were disappointed by the Allied decision in 1919 to give them only part of what they claimed. Even this part is not justified by their numerical strength. The total population of Czecho-Slovakia is about 14,500,000, not more than half of whom are Czechs. The rest is composed of national minorities on whom Czech rule was imposed by force.

The artificial existence of Czecho-Slovakia came into being in the Conference chamber and resulted in one-half of its population being placed in the position of ruler over the other half; a rule which they have since exercised by means of force and, on occasions, terror. The Czechs' ruling position is not due to their own superior power or ability, nor has it any historical justification; it is due solely to the fact of their having committed high treason during the War, by offering their services to the Allies, who were the declared enemies of their own properly constituted government, and to the fact that they formed a strategical outpost for France in her latent conflict with the Germans.

The European Chancellories have known anxious hours during the last few months. The Czech question, even more than that of the Spanish Civil War, has darkened the political horizon of Europe.

Many in England have thrown the blame for the dangers implicit in the situation on Czecho-Slovakia's most powerful neighbour, but there is no real evidence of ill-intent on the part of that neighbour. On the contrary, it is the Czechs who have multiplied their provocations of Germany during recent months. This has only been made possible by Prague's belief in the certainty of French and Soviet support. The Czechs still cherish illusions as to the possibility of a future based on the documents and maps referred to earlier. In endeavouring to understand Czech mentality it must always be remembered that this State, negligible in size though it is, is swollen with Imperialistic ambitions and an unceasing urge towards ever wider expansion. Political cartoonists usually represent Czecho-Slovakia as a small boy with an immensely swollen head... and are not far wide of the mark.

3

Composition of
Czecho-Slovakia's Population

The official census of 1930 shows Czecho-Slovakia to possess some 14,500,000 citizens, of whom only 7,400,000 are Czech. Details are furnished later on in this book tending to prove that even this Czech figure is exaggerated. It suffices for the moment to accept Prague's own official figures. These show that the Czechs number 51.2% of the whole population. In considering this alleged fact it must be remembered that the census was not carried out in accordance with the tongue of the various peoples but rather on the basis of previous registration of nationality and that Czech officials were in a position to influence its results by the "gentle persuasion" they were able to exercise on the various minorities with a view to convincing them of the desirability of acquiring Czech nationality; the fact of this pressure has never been denied. The unreliability of a census of this nature is self-evident. In a case of this kind the secrecy is as essential as it is in that secret ballot which is one of the main achievements of democracy. The absence of any secrecy from the 1930 census would lead one to believe that the Czech element was not exactly under-estimated.

There are 2,300,000 Slovaks to be added to the Czechs, again taking official figures.

Ethnographically speaking the Slovaks are related to the Czechs but are by no means of the same race. It will thus be seen that Czecho-Slovakia is in reality a conglomeration of Czech, Slovak, Hungarian, German, Ruthenian and other component parts. The principle of self-determination has been admitted in the case of all other European minorities, and it seems a little inconsistent to deny it to those of Czecho-Slovakia.

According to the official census of 1930 the Germans with 3,300,000, or 22.3%, form the largest of the non-Slav minorities. There were in that year, 692,000 Hungarians and 13,000 Rumanians, from whose number 187,000 persons registered as Jews were excluded; 550,000 Russians or Ruthenians and 81,000 Poles go to swell the Slav elements.

It will therefore be seen that the official census shows Czecho-Slovakia to be a compound of nationalities having a Slav core with many non-Slav offshoots. The Czechs admit the legal existence of the German minority and - as mentioned above - officially list them at 3,300,000. It must be taken into consideration, however, that of the total German population in Czecho-Slovakia, almost 3 million live in definitely German territory covering some 30,000 sq. kms., which follows the German frontier. This stretch of land begins at Lundenburg, passing Znaim on the Austrian border to Bohemian-Krumau, Prachatitz (Prachatice), Bischofteinitz, Marienbad, Eger, Carlsbad, Saaz, Lobositz, and Leitmeritz to the east and south, respectively, of Bavaria and Saxony, finally curving round to the south of the Reich Province of Silesia. It is characterized by the typical German cities of Reichenberg, Gablonz, Moravian-Trübau, Zwittau, Landskron, Neutitschein. According to official Czech figures, this territory harbours 334,000 Czechs, constituting roughly only 11% of the total population. It is known, however, that in these statistics Germans with a working knowledge of Czech are listed as Czechs and that the figures are greatly altered in favour of the German element if the Austrian statistics of 1910, which are closer to actual conditions, are taken as a basis.

The only true German minorities are those in the districts round Brunn and Iglau and those Germans living in Carpathia.

The foregoing facts supply all the explanation needed for the demand made by the Sudeten Germans of full equality of status with the Czechs. This equality must include recognition of German territorial inviolability, that is to say, the cessation of attempted denationalization in German-speaking areas. The importance of this proviso can be seen when it is realized that there were 25% more Czech officials in German areas in 1930 than there were in 1921, while the percentage of Germans in the whole population of German-speaking areas has decreased markedly in the same period. (See Table I, Appendix.)

Official figures, unreliable as they are, take us no farther than 1930. To-day's position can, however, be guessed at from the recent municipal elections which took place under the system of secret balloting, as is usual in all democratic countries, and may be taken as a reasonable indication of the real state of public opinion.

There were elections in 2,737 German-speaking communities; in 1,456 of these the Sudeten German candidates were returned unopposed, voting was therefore confined to 1,281 communities which correspond roughly to English boroughs. The Press of Czecho-Slovakia has not published the total figures of votes cast, in the obvious wish to emphasize the purely municipal character of the election. In accordance with that wish, local figures alone were given. It is impossible to obtain a comprehensive view of the results since each of a multiplicity of local papers was the sole carrier of its own local figures. It is true that the Sudeten German Press published a comprehensive survey of their own successes, but this was estimated in a percentage of German votes, instead of a percentage of national votes. It is, however, possible to form a reasonable idea of the results as a whole.

The first group of municipal elections returned Sudeten German candidates unopposed in 16 out of 69 German communities. In the case of the other 53 districts the Press published exceptionally the total of votes recorded: of a voting population of 172,553, 137,358 cast their votes in favour of the German party. Of the purely German votes the Sudeten German party obtained 121,891, or almost 90%. Of the total, 28,301 votes were given to the Czechs, a proportion of some 17%; the Communists succeeded in obtaining 6,894 only, or 4%. Election results in the larger districts are given in Table III of the Appendix. In the remaining 46 communities Germans polled 70,868 votes, out of a total of 82,233 recorded, leaving to Czechs and Communists combined a scant 14% of the whole. The census of 1930 gives Brüx and Dux a very mixed ethnography. Since those days the lignite pits have brought many Czech miners to the district.

The second stage gave 373 communities to Henlein's men without a contest; elections took place in 347 communities. The markedly anti-German *Prager Tageblatt* estimated the German percentage of all votes cast as from 80-85% and is hardly likely to have erred on the side of ex-aggeration. It is a fact that the Sudeten German party polled 290,015 of the 317,405 German votes recorded. Election results of the two largest towns, Gablonz and Komotau, can be seen in Table IV. There is no need to quote further results, the high percentage of the whole clearly showing the size of the majority in the unmixed areas. The Sudeten German party polled almost 80% of the total votes cast in Eastern Bohemia.

In the final stages 1,948 German communities went to the polling booths; 1,003 of these returned only Sudeten German candidates, while of the 824,282 German votes cast Henlein's party obtained 749,820. The election results of the larger towns may be seen in Table VI. Apart from Iglau, which has always had a very mixed population, a comparison of the Czech vote in 1935 with the same vote in 1938 is proof of the great influx of Czechs which has taken place in German-speaking areas during that period. There was an increase of 2,891 Czech votes in Iglau and 1,263 in Troppau over the corresponding figures in 1935. Czech votes increased by 599 in Saaz, in Leitmeritz by 499, to mention only two large centres where the Czech population has grown. As, however, all votes lost by the Social Democrats went to swell the total of the Sudeten German party, that party's majority was retained.

The increase of their votes in Troppau was 3,896, while the combined Social Democratic and Communist totals were lessened by only 552. In Leitmeritz the Left wing lost 154 votes, while the Sudetens increased their poll by 1,078. The German *enclave* of Stecken was carried by the Czechs, whose representation rose from eight to ten seats, the Germans losing two of their previous ten. The Czech invasion is reflected by the increased representation of their parties. In some twenty districts Czechs obtained an additional number of seats. As the nomination of deputy-mayors is entrusted to a minority, not less than 25%, by the electoral law, and as the German Social Democrats threw in their lot with Czechs and Communists against the Sudetens, a Czech will, for the first time, be seen as deputy-mayor in Troppau and probably in Saaz.

4

Minority Concerns

While it is true that the German Democratic party is in opposition to the Sudeten German party as regards local politics, they are at one with them in so far as concerned their common national policy. M. Wenzel Jaksch, leader of the Democrats, stated at a meeting at Bodenbach on April 26th, 1936:

> "Ever since 1918 the fundamental problem of the co-operation of the various nationalities which go to make up the Czecho-Slovakian State has either been ignored or treated unilaterally. The Czechs claim to have fulfilled their obligations towards the minorities, but this is not so. Properly to understand our importance as a minority it must not be forgotten that there are in Europe to-day several independent States whose total populations are less than the total of the Sudeten Germans. Czech statesmen must make up their minds as to whether there is a place for the Sudeten Germans in the Republic."

The dwindling enthusiasm for Communism provides the Sudeten German party with a reserve of potential converts, but since the Communist party knows no nationality, many of these converts must necessarily transfer their allegiance to the Czechs. The *Prager Tageblatt* estimates that two-thirds of the Communist party in German-speaking areas are Germans. The German political group may well be strengthened, as opposed to the Czech group, by the conversion of Left wing adherents. But a legal embargo of the denationalization of German areas is none the less necessary. National territoriality was laid down as one of the essential conditions of the Czech constitution. Unhappily this condition has been repeatedly and constantly infringed. For example, the postmasters in the German towns of Asch and Schönbach are Czechs. Transference of Czech officials to German-speaking areas and, conversely, of German officials to Czech districts, is a favourite method of German denationalization; a new principle is needed, only German officials in German areas and *vice versa*. If the official use of their own language is granted to minorities of not less than 15% by the new language law, many German areas will become bilingual. *The Times* of December 2nd, 1937, summed up the position as follows:

> *"The Czechs refuse to allow the German language to be treated on a footing of equality with their own."*

The Hungarian minority was also left with a grievance by the Treaty of Trianon; an area 63,000 kilometres square containing a population estimated at 1,870,000 in 1910 was ceded to Czecho-Slovakia. Of this total about 800,000 Hungarians lived in a compact area comprising less than a fifth of the whole.

The first official Czech census took place in 1921; 738,516 Hungarians only were recorded, of whom 634,827 lived in Slovakia while 103,690 were recorded in the Carpathian area. These figures point to the mysterious disappearance of over 30% of the Hungarian population between 1910 and 1921. By a strange coincidence the population shown as belonging to the Czecho-Slovak group increased by an almost exactly similar percentage. While it is true that many Hungarians fled the country on the formation of the Czech Republic, yet many returned later; in any case, the official figures give the total of these emigrants as 106,841 between 1918 and 1914. These were mainly dismissed ex-Government officials and political offenders.

A "Conscription" census was held in the Slovak areas in 1919; the Hungarian population was shown as having fallen by 203,000. This census took place for the purpose of preparing military service lists; consequently the Prague authorities desired a minimum of Hungarians.

Various other official figures published in Prague show that the number of Hungarians is still declining.

Census papers in Czecho-Slovakia are filled in in a different manner to that customary in this country, where the head of the household does the work himself. In Czecho-Slovakia the task is entrusted to special commissioners. In the Slovak census referred to there were 14,100 of these commissioners of whom only 594 were Hungarians. On the basis of the previous census the Hungarian minority were entitled to over 3,000 commissioners of their own nationality. There is evidence to prove that many of these commissioners used pencils in filling up the forms; this method makes possible, to say the least of it, subsequent alteration. In many cases householders were not allowed to see the completed forms and so could not tell whether the details supplied by them were entered as given. Many of the officials spoke no Hungarian, which must have made matters somewhat complicated. Hungarian Jews and gypsies were set down as Jews or gypsies without qualification of nationality, though their only tongue was Hungarian. Czech ancestry, however slight, automatically rendered a Hungarian Czech. In an English census this might be compared to entering as French any English persons of Norman ancestry.

The alteration of population ratios established by the census is shown in [Appendix] Table A. In comparison with 1910 Hungarian figures in the Pressburg-Pozsony area fell from 40%-16% while the corresponding Czech figure rose from 14%-51%. Though 38% of the population of Kashau was Hungarian in 1919, by 1930 these figures had fallen to 18%. During the same period Czecho-Slovakian figures rose from 14%-66%; this in spite of the fact that fifteen out of forty-eight elected Town

Councillors were members of Hungarian parties and fourteen more were Hungarian by extraction. The Hungarian population of Uzhorod fell by 62%, while the Czecho-Slovaks increased by 24%.

Devious means were employed by the Czech authorities in order to decrease the apparent proportions. The 1921 census showed that 20% of the population in the Pressburg area was Hungarian. In order to lessen this proportion the authorities resorted to cleavage, adding sixteen Hungarian communities to the neighbouring Galanta area and replacing them by non-Hungarian communities from the Bazin area.

By virtue of the fact that a minimum proportion of 20% was necessary in order that a minority should enjoy the right to use their own tongue for all purposes these two areas were deprived of this right. The same treatment was meted out to Hungarian minorities in Kashau, Nyitra and Rimaszombat.

Further reductions in Hungarian figures were recorded by the census of 1930. There has been a fall in Hungarian figures in several agricultural areas where it can be proved that no emigration whatever has taken place; this reduction, amounting to as much as 15%, is purely a paper one, caused by administrative action.

After the elections of 1930 the Pressburg results were challenged, the presiding authorities being accused of falsification.

During the municipal elections this summer great activity was displayed by the Hungarian parties. (See Table B, Appendix, for population figures.)

5

Ruthenia

The narrow *enclave* in the extreme east of Czecho-Slovakia bordered on the north-east by Poland, on the south-west by Hungary, and on the south by Rumania is known as Ruthenia. It is often referred to by the Prague Government as Carpathian Russia though the inhabitants are no more nearly related to the Russians than they are to the Czechs. These Ruthenians, or Ukrainians, are of quite separate blood; their manners and customs differ widely from those of Russia.

Ruthenia is a country possessing a very distinct individuality of its own. Official figures published in 1933 show that of a total population of 685,000, 624,000 were indigenous Ukrainians. The remaining 61,000 was made up of 30,000 Jews, 20,000 Hungarians, and some 10,000 Germans. Inasmuch as Ruthenia is a completely self-contained province it seems a little difficult to understand why its government should be entrusted to Czechs.

Consciousness of nationality is of comparatively recent growth among the Ruthenian population; in fact, it may be said that its rise has only become apparent during the last ten years. The Ruthenians are small farmers in the main. Prior to 1918 they formed part of the Austro-Hungarian monarchy; consequently the formation of the new republic meant only to them the substitution of one foreign overlord for another. Their dormant feelings of nationalism were aroused by Czech ill-treatment.

Ruthenian inclusion in the Czecho-Slovak State was announced on May 8th, 1919. The Ukraine, or Ruthenia, as it was now called, had never any relations with the Czechs; no historical nor ethnographical reasons can be adduced in support of this inclusion. Nevertheless, the Ruthenian Congress held at Scranton, Penn., on November 19th, 1918, decided to throw in their lot with Czecho-Slovakia on a federal and autonomist footing. The Treaty of St. Germain confirmed the rights of the Ukrainians, giving them local self-government by their own elective Diet, having jurisdiction over all religious, educational and language questions. It was also expressly laid down that Ruthenian officials were, in as far as possible, to be of Ruthenian blood. The Czech authorities, however, succeeded in postponing this autonomy on the grounds that the country was not ripe for self-government and would require at least twenty years of tutelage.

A further breach of the Peace Treaty was committed in 1926, when the official language of the country was declared to be Czech. The Ruthenians by this act, indefensible as it was, lost their last illusions as to the Republic's good faith. Their voluntary union with Czecho-Slovakia had been conditioned by the promised grant of autonomy. No part of this autonomy had been granted, in fact, with the minor exception of the appointment of a Ruthenian Governor. This apparently important concession has always been tendered more or less void by the selection as governors of men notorious for their weakness of character. In almost every case these Governors have been under the thumb of their Czech Deputy Governors. The present Deputy Governor, M. Meznik, is a particularly intransigent Czech whose desire to absorb Ruthenia is well known; he has been in office for the past three years.

Over 40,000 Czechs have been introduced into the Ukraine since 1919. Revenue administration to the extent of 98% of the local officials is in the hands of the Czechs.

The Czech Premier in March, 1937, promised autonomy to "Carpathian Russia" in the terms of the Treaty signed at St. Germain en Laye.

On April 4th, 1937, a bill was put forward whose ostensible aim was Ukrainian local self-government. This Bill was duly passed in spite of the protests of the Ruthenian deputies. Other minority members also went into the Opposition lobbies. This opposition rose from the fact that for the promised Diet was substituted an advisory council.

Of the twenty-four members allotted to this Council no less than nine were to be Czech governmental nominees. This pretence of autonomy was rejected by a M. Fensik, the Ruthenian leader, as valueless.

Ukrainian discontent in the face of Czech immigration had been on the increase for some considerable time; this disappointment of their cherished hopes of self-government brought it to a climax.

The Ukrainians began to organize politically in 1928 and 1929. Of the 300 Ukrainian students at the University of Prague in 1929 only ninety were identified with the Ukrainian political party; this figure had risen to 230 by 1937.

The Czechs use the Ukraine as the Russians use Siberia. Inept officials and those guilty of misdemeanours, together with those who for some reason or another have fallen under official displeasure, are banished to the Ukraine. This hardly makes for the better government of that province.

It is symptomatic that very close contact is maintained by Czecho-Slovakia's Ukrainians with their compatriots on the other side of the Carpathians.

The Union of Ruthenian teachers is solidly Ukrainian in politics. Fourteen hundred out of their 1,800 members proclaimed their adherence to national ideals in 1931, when they passed a resolution desiring the abolition of the name "Carpathian Russia" to be met with a flat refusal by Prague. The fight for nationality is now being waged in the schools. Imposition of a bastard Carpatho-Russian language has long been attempted by the Central authorities, although it bears as little relation to Ruthenian as does Dutch to English. Ukrainian school books were printed in this language, and in a script which is a mixture between ecclesiastical and normal Russian alphabets. This script, not unnaturally, aroused the greatest discontent. Parents refused to allow their children to attend schools using these books and demanded that their own tongue should be used. Last Christmas a plebiscite was held on the question. The Czechs promised that areas polling more than 50% of the votes cast in favour of Ukrainian should have the language they desired. The results of the plebiscite in the various areas showed an average of 85% of the whole in favour of Ukrainia. Prague thereupon declared the plebiscite null and void. In February of this year another plebiscite was held under the strict supervision of specially imported Czech police. The Ukrainians are a simple people, easily terrorised; many voted consequently in favour of the alien tongue. With the departure of the police came repentance; sporadic and endemic school strikes took place. It should be remembered that Ruthenia contains a small number of true Russians, immigrants from their own country who have become settlers in the Czech Ukraine. Since the Ukrainian teachers were not conversant with the synthetic alphabet used in the new school books some of these were appointed in their place; the schools over which they presided were boycotted.

The Ukrainian Press has only been in existence for a matter of weeks. In the whole of Czecho-Slovakia the Ukraine possessed no newspaper of its own until May 15th of this year. The Ukraine, poverty-stricken as it is, managed to collect the relatively amazing sum of 21,000 Czech crowns. With this money a paper was started; its name is *Nowa Sloboda*. Since then a second newspaper, run by the Ukrainians, has come into being. There is also an opposition journal published in the Ukraine whose policy is anti-national; its list of subscribers this summer amounted to as many as 136. A newspaper with a subscription list of such a size can hardly claim to be self-supporting.

The Ukrainians have started an institute of national education, among whose departments are to be found libraries and which hold educational courses all over the province. There is a branch whose business is the encouragement of dramatic and musical art. Ukrainian folk plays arouse much enthusiasm. There is a Ruthenian national theatre where performances are given to full houses; Prague has recently founded a Russian theatre but its performances are only sparsely attended.

The Ukraine is mainly an agricultural and pastoral country, whose inhabitants are country rather than town dwellers; trade in the towns is largely in the hands of the Jewish community. The Ukrainians are a friendly race who take a great interest in all forms of sport. Association football is their favourite game, though they have produced some internationally well-known tennis players. The Boy Scout movement is making great progress.

Relations between the native population of the Ukraine and the few thousand German settlers are of the best. The Ukraine owes an architectural debt to these alien immigrants, for the beautiful Gothic cathedral at Bardijov was erected to the design of a German in the seventeenth century, when the town in question had an almost exclusively German population.

Their acknowledged failure to absorb the Ukrainians into the Czech race has caused the latter to adopt the method of treating inhabitants of Ruthenia as Russians - a method which arouses the strongest resentment. Had it not been for the stupid and provocative nature of Czech rule, the Ukrainians, whose main desire is to live a peaceful life; would no doubt have been content with their subservient position for many years to come. Consciousness of nationality has been brought to the surface by persistent ill-treatment and supremely tactless methods. The present-day unrest is entirely due to the inability of the Czech mentality to appreciate the views and desires of peoples other than their own.

6

The Polish Minority

There is a compact Polish minority in Czecho-Slovakia on the Polish frontier consisting of the Freistadt and Cesky districts. While official figures show a high proportion of Czechs in these areas their voting strength is, remarkably enough, comparatively insignificant. This fact scarcely tends to strengthen one's faith in Prague's official statistics (Ref. Table C). An example of such statistics may be seen by reference to the town of Lomna Dolna. In 1921, 94.2% of the population were Poles. The figures given by Prague for 1930 reduce this percentage to 67.4; this statement is, to say the least of it, somewhat unconvincing. Many districts in the area had a population more than 50% Polish in 1921.

It is difficult to understand why these areas were allotted to Czecho-Slovakia at the time of the creation of that State. Mr. Lloyd George, in the course of a series of articles in *The Daily Telegraph* in July this year, wrote:

> *"President Benes drew attention to the exposed situation of the Czecho-Slovak nation as the advance-guard of the Slav world in the West and therefore constantly threatened by German expansion."*

Oppression of Polish, Slovak and Ukrainian minorities all of whom are claimed to be of Slav origin, by the Czechs, hardly bears out M. Benes' claim on behalf of the "Czecho-Slovak nation" to the position of "advance-guard of the Slav world." It would appear that the only Slavs in modern Europe whom the Czechs are not in a position to oppress are the fortunate citizens of the Soviet paradise. One can only presume that M. Benes regards his country as the advance-guard of the U.S.S.R.

It is remarkable that the menace of German expansion was conjured up at the moment of Germany's complete disarmament when she was in possession of neither war-craft nor aeroplanes and her prospected collapse appeared to be more probable than any chance of expansion.

However that may be, Prague obtained the Polish areas. Czech official figures in 1921 placed the number of Poles in the Republic at 23,562 plus a number of Poles who had obtained voluntary and Czech naturalization, making a grand total of 92,529. In addition to this there are 25,000 other Poles whom the Czech authorities classify as "Silesian Czechs." On the other hand, Warsaw claims that there were 118,000 Poles in Silesia in 1921. They state that there were 112,000 Poles among the 205,000 inhabitants of Freistadt and Tesin, giving a proportion of 54%, as against the Prague figures of 30%. The rest of Czecho-Slovakia seems to have contained upwards of 137,000 Poles in 1921, if one ignores their paper nationality. Nor must we forget the 9,000 odd Poles in Moravia. In the years that have passed since 1921 the population of the Polish-speaking areas shows a large increase; consequently the Polish minority is larger than generally believed. The Polish minority, in common with all the other minorities, is gravely discontented. They have no liking for their position as "the advance-guard of the Slav world." Quite on the contrary they view with no favour the close relations of "their" Government with Moscow, and would prefer to be merely Poles.

7

The Men at the Helm

A survey of the personalities and characters of some of the leading protagonists in the troubled politics of Czecho-Slovakia may not be without interest.

The Premier, M. Hodza, is a professor. It seems to be Czecho-Slovakia's fate to be ruled by men of academic attainments. Masaryk was a professor and Benes only just failed to become one.

Hodza is well known as a man of letters. Son of a Protestant divine, he was born at Sucany. He devoted his time to the study of history and became professor of modern Slav history at the University of Pressburg. By birth he is a Slovak. His family has an interesting tradition. His uncle, Michael Miloslav Hodza, was one of the leaders against Hungarian oppression in 1848. His views have greatly influenced his nephew, who became a member of the Hungarian House of Representatives in 1910. He was a Democrat politically, whose policy was mainly directed at the liberation of what he called the "oppressed minorities" from the rule of the Hapsburgs. He established a close connexion between the Czech, Rumanian and Yugo-Slav Democratic parties. At the same time he was, however, a close friend of that Dr. Vajdas who enjoyed the confidence of the Archduke Franz Ferdinand, a liberal-minded prince who planned to transform the Dual Monarchy into a federation of national states. He it was who fell victim to assassination at Serajevo.

Hodza's moment came with the creation of the Republic of Czecho-Slovakia. There is no doubt that his country's politics had not always been in accordance with his own personal views. He is avowedly an agrarian and has voiced ideas on more than one occasion aiming at the creation of an agrarian *bloc* in Central Europe balanced by a consumers' group formed by the Western industrial Powers. He is out of touch with M. Benes' socialist principles, nor does he favour the Liberal side. As regards domestic politics he is a declared enemy of Bolshevism and is not in full agreement with the present trend of foreign policy in its relations with Moscow. He is a Slovak, first and foremost, and a believer in the ultimate close union of Czechs and Slovaks. It is his view that the Czechs do not need the Slovaks so much as the Slovaks need the Czechs. When he joined the Czechs in 1918 it was, perhaps, without giving sufficient consideration to the true national aspirations and wants of his own people.

He himself has been successful enough, for capable brains are to seek in Prague. Hodza will always be necessary to the Central Government on account of his intimate knowledge of the Hungarian problem. He was posted to Budapest as Ambassador in 1918 and led the Czech Mission there during the Rumanian occupation of that capital. He was at the head of various Ministries as time went on, first at the Home Office, then at the Ministry of Education, and later at the Ministry of Agriculture. Governments rose and fell, but he was always a member of them. On November 5th, 1935, he became Premier, being the first Slovak to reach that position. He has not had an easy task. During his Premiership the Slovak People's party has greatly increased its strength under the leadership of the aged cleric, the late Rev. Father Hlinka, who was regarded as the apostolic father of his people, and whose Separatist policy of secession by Slovakia from the remainder of the hybrid state is meeting with more and more approval day by day. When he was Minister of Education, some years ago, Hodza proposed a policy of co-operation with Germany, but was over-ruled by his colleagues in the Cabinet. Only recently he declared: "We need peace with Germany and must have it, irrespective of her form of government." Only a few days after that speech tension between Prague and Berlin became acute, owing to the misguided action of some of his collaborators. As Prime Minister, Hodza has had a hard row to hoe. He has given evidence of great ability on many occasions and is a man of character and decision. His present responsibilities are of the greatest, and it may well be that on him depends the issue of peace or war in Europe.

Edward Benes, President of Czecho-Slovakia, is looked upon as a fixed star in his country's firmament. Ever since 1916 he has played the same instrument in the concert of Europe. He, too, is a man of great ability and takes his life's work in the most serious manner.

This is perhaps in part due to the fact that peasant blood runs in his veins. He was born in the village of Korlany near Kralovice in West Bohemia, on May 28th, 1884. His parents' scanty means just permitted them to send him to college in Prague, where he showed much interest in social and political problems at an early age. He took up the study of law and political economy later at the Czech University in Prague. His tutor was none other than Thomas Masaryk, who had held the chair of philosophy since 1882 and who included political economy among the subjects of his lectures.

Benes found himself in disagreement with his tutor on many points, one of which was the relative importance of the nationalities question as the primary problem of the Czech State. But they had a national ideal in common and became friends. Benes went to work with a view to the dissolution of the old Dual Monarchy. In his endeavours to interest foreign personages he visited, among other places, Paris, London and Berlin. He got his degree of philosophy at Prague in 1908, entitling him, as is the local custom, to the qualification of *Doctor*. Shortly after this he became a tutor of political economy at the Czech Commercial School. In 1912 he published a pamphlet dealing with the history of political parties; he was later awarded the title of *Professor*. He was in the habit of contributing articles to Socialist papers and, among his other activities, translated one of Zola's novels. It was not long after the outbreak of War before he left his native country. It was his belief that the way to the formation of a Czech national state led over the ruins of the Hapsburg Empire; he deserted to the Allies, where he found himself in company with his old friend Masaryk. At the outset of their relationship the Allies viewed the idea of a national state put forward by the two Czechs with little favour, for they had in mind the perpetuation of the Dual Monarchy, though in a truncated form. Benes made himself responsible for Press propaganda and extended the activities of the Slav Press Bureau, which Masaryk had established in London. This Bureau later became the Czech Embassy. Benes contributed to the British and French Press and was responsible on more than one occasion for the publication of Austrian secret documents. He let no grass grow under his feet during the War years. He was rewarded by an almost complete success, coincident with the collapse of the old Dual Monarchy. When the first professional Czech Government was formed on November 14th, 1918, Edward Benes was one of its leaders, and was the best-known Czech after Masaryk. It was he who claimed the status of a Great Power for his country, a claim which he has since pursued regardless of the rights or feelings of other nationalities. It was his eloquent voice which persuaded President Wilson to give his vote for the revocation of the autonomy previously granted to the Sudeten Germans. It was in gratitude for this support that the Czechs named a railway station after Wilson. Hungarian, Slovak, Ruthenian and Polish minorities met with similar treatment. Benes was the main instrument in the creation of "Greater Czecho-Slovakia" and the instigator of the oppressive treatment of the minorities.

He was at the Ministry for Foreign Affairs in fourteen different Governments during seventeen years and also held the post of Premier in one of them. He is a well-known figure at European Conferences.

Acquisition is easy; the maintenance of what one has acquired is more difficult. Benes gave his country wide territories, but only at the expense of other nationalities. At Geneva he forged the links of the chain which connects Prague with France and Soviet Russia. As everybody knows he became President after the death of Masaryk. Since his elevation to the presidential chair he has struggled more vigorously than ever to maintain Czech supremacy at any cost, even to the extent of a general European War.

Once leader of the Sudeten Party only, Konrad Henlein is now the acknowledged leader of the whole German-speaking minority. Oppression rose to such a pitch in 1933 that all the German parties, with the exception of small groups of little importance, began to unite under his leadership. In an impassioned speech he once quoted the words that Masaryk wrote in *The World Revolution*:

> *"The Germans cannot be considered as second-class citizens amongst as. On the contrary, they were invited by our Kings to our country in Mediaeval times on account of their colonizing abilities. They were guaranteed full rights and everything necessary to their cultural and national life by Royal Decree."*

Henlein was just thirty-six years of age when he made that speech, which was to be the start of his political mission. He was then a gymnastic instructor at Asch. He had no easy beginning, for the other German parties were unwilling to acknowledge him at first, while the Czechs regarded him, as they still do, with the gravest mistrust.

He founded his own party on October 1st, 1933. A month later he had 7,000 adherents when he addressed a meeting at Reichenberg. By July, 1934, his audiences had grown to 15,000 and since then have been many times multiplied. Sixty thousand enthusiastic listeners heard him speak at Haida on September 1st, 1935, and he addressed upwards of 100,000 at Teplitz on October 20th in the same year.

He is now the sole leader of those who flock to his standard. At the elections in May, 1935, the Sudeten German party polled over 1,750,000 votes, leaving a negligible quantity of votes to be divided among all the other parties. At Braunau on September 23rd, 1936, Henlein averred, "We are no longer a party, we have become a whole people." The

Czechs tried to stem the rising tide of German nationalism by inviting representatives of the negligible German opposition groups to take part in the Government, but without any effect on the situation. On April 5th, 1934, Henlein developed his views for an assembly of politicians, economists and representatives of the Press. They were, in principle, the same as the now famous Karlsbad Eight Points Demand of April 23rd, 1938. His claim to national self-government for his own Germans does not necessarily mean the dissolution of Czecho-Slovakia. All he asks are fair and just conditions for the German-speaking minority.

He paid his first visit to friends in England in July, 1937, and came to London again in May of this year. Mr. Garvin, in an issue of The Observer, at that time stated that Czecho-Slovakia was faced with the choice between dissolution and a federal system.

What has happened since then is known to all the world. Henlein has been engaged as unfettered representative of the Sudeten Germans in long and usually abortive discussions with the Prague Government. He and Hodza have met on many occasions. Henlein is strong in his determination to obtain fair treatment for the German minority and has shown conspicuous ability as a negotiator.

The Slovaks are without a leader since the death of their beloved Father Hlinka. He never looked upon his people as a minority but rather as a nation, and once referred in a speech to "the sovereign people of Slovakia." Under the terms of the Pittsburg Agreement, which was signed on May 30th, 1918, in the American town which gives it its name, the Slovaks were granted rights of absolute equality with the Czechs. Masaryk was amongst those who signed it.

In practice the Slovak question has become another minority problem, owing to the overbearing nature of the Czech mentality. Though it is true, as we have already seen, that the present Premier is a Slovak, he is faced by almost insurmountable difficulties.

Father Hlinka was called the Slovak Apostle. He aimed at absolute freedom for his people. Hodza, who is undoubtedly if subconsciously influenced by his Czech associations, thinks, on the other hand, in terms of helping his countrymen to rise to the Czech cultural level.

Father Hlinka was a very remarkable man. He came of peasant stock and was born in 1864. In accordance with his parents' wish he entered the Roman Catholic priesthood. The Slovak are a sincerely religious people and found in their leader an object for veneration. Indeed, the less educated sections of the populace regarded him as something more than human, a state of affairs which he was the last man to desire. His tastes were simple, his life austere, and this was perhaps partly responsible for the reverence with which his fellow-countrymen regard him.

He was an idealist who struggled for many years to win independence for his people; at one time he was imprisoned by the Hungarians on this account. He was a man of great learning and performed the colossal task of translating both the Old and the New Testament into his mother tongue. He was the prime mover of the formation of many organizations and founded two newspapers, *The Daily Slovak* and *The Weekly Review, Tatransky Slovak*. Increasing age and the ravages of illness were unable to cut short his activities, which only terminated with his recent death.

He did much during his lifetime to make Slovakia's point of view understood by the world. In particular, he won much sympathy in Poland, where in 1919 he discussed his people's aspirations with Marshal Pilsudski. The original of the Pittsburg Agreement came to him in the spring of this year through the good offices of Warsaw.

Czech opposition to the reasonable desires of Slovakia is hard to understand. During Father Hlinka's lifetime repeated attempts were made by Prague to induce their priestly opponent to retire, and bribes in the shape of promises of future action were offered to him on several occasions, to be met with his resolute refusal.

The production of the Pittsburg Agreement in course of the Congress of the Slovak People's party at Pressburg, came as a complete surprise to Prague. Masaryk's signature, in particular, produced a considerable revulsion of feeling, for Masaryk is a national hero. Hlinka stated regretfully: "Every nationality of the State we have to found and support has sent us loyal and fraternal greetings on the occasion of our celebration - the Germans, the Hungarians, the Poles and the Ruthenians - only the Czechs have held aloof."

Father Hlinka's recent death comes as a tragic reminder of the frequency with which human aspirations are only fulfilled after the departure of their maker. Father Hlinka will long be remembered among the fellow-countrymen who revered him, and those Europeans who had come to look upon this devoted priest with feelings of admiration.

Dr. Hletko, the leader of the Slovaks in America, travelled all the way from the United States to his old homeland to help support Hlinka in his heroic fight. Americans of Slovak extraction saved their dimes for the aged Slovak priest who was, as official representative of his people, refused admission to the Paris Peace Conference when the Czech boundaries were fixed, and whose one aim was to free his suffering people before he closed his eyes for ever....

Hletko's mission was supported by tens of thousands of Slovaks overseas; and when the time came - in August, 1938 - for him to return to the States, there were heartrending scenes. In a final address to his comrades, Hletko said:

> "We have thoroughly investigated the conditions, and must say that the complaints of the Slovaks in the Republic are completely justified. Your fight is right, and you must struggle still harder. We shall support you from America by the sharpest action.
>
> "Slovak America goes into the arena just as it did twenty years ago. Our leader! Slovak America is behind you! May God grant that you may long be spared to lead the Slovak people!"

Hlinka responded as follows:

> "...I do not know if we should still exist without your help. We must still fight here, for the right and might which should be in

the hands of the Slovak people are not in their possession. We will not bend our knees.... We have a clear goal, and we Slovaks are to-day united."

Hletko gave a farewell address at Rosenberg, adding that the American Slovaks considered it right for their countrymen to be good friends with the Poles, Magyars and Germans.

Many Slovaks were in tears as Hletko departed by way of Poland for the States. But they looked grim, even in their grief. For they were determined to continue the fight, and Hlinka, their leader, was with them. One could see this aged priest without a pang. Despite his years, he was in the front rank of the Slovak army behind the banner of freedom, determined to gain his people's independence. For twenty years he had accused Prague. For twenty years he had been the apostle of freedom among the Slovaks. And with old age overtaking him, he still saw his goal clearly, and devoted the evening of his life to the welfare of his down-trodden fellow-countrymen. He will go down to history as one of the pioneers of real freedom, who grew old struggling against the might of oppression. For Hlinka has become an historical personage. He died shortly after the visit of the American Slovak leader at the age of 74. In Rosenberg, where he closed his eyes for ever, the church bells rang as soon as the news became known. Bad news proverbially spreads quickly, and soon the surrounding areas, finally the whole of Slovakia, sounded the mourning bells for the dead leader. His mortal remains were embalmed and he was buried in the local cemetery for the time being. A mausoleum is to be built for him, and the Slovaks will later transfer him to this.

Fifty thousand men and women accompanied the dead priest to the grave. All prominent Slovaks, including Premier Hodza, attended his funeral, while Poland, Rumania, and all the nationalities in the Czech Republic sent representatives. The railway station of Rosenberg was draped in black and green, while black-draped notices announced: "Hlinka is dead!"

One might imagine that this aged priest, who had held office in Rosenberg since the 'nineties, would have been immune from brutal attacks. And one might have assumed, at least, that his burial would not be an excuse for hard words. This was not so. Hlinka wanted the freedom promised his people after the War. And so the Czech Press published the most objectionable obituary notices one can imagine. The *Ranni Noviny,* for example, wrote:

> *"Although Hlinka was a fanatical Roman Catholic priest, he had nothing priestly about him. It is hard to say what drove him to such a shallow, empty opposition. The real reason appears to have been his personal vanity and longing for fame...."*

This about a man who suffered imprisonment on many occasions for his fellow-countrymen, and who lived the simplest of simple lives, who was, apart from that, ailing for some time before his death. I was unable to interview him some months ago when in his home town, because of his bad state of health. His recovery was more apparent than real in the weeks preceding his death.

Other Czech papers reported similarly. The *Ceské Skovo* referred to his "selfish interests," as did several other journals.

The Slovaks have suffered a heavy loss in Hlinka, but their movement is too strong to disappear. Hlinka's successors are carrying the fight on, and Hlinka's memory will spur them onwards. His life was devoted to two aims only - to the Church, which he served so long, and to his Slovak people, for whose freedom he fought uninterruptedly from decade to decade, under the old Dual Monarchy, as well as under the rule of the present Czecho-Slovakian Republic.

There were pathetic scenes at his funeral. Strong men burst into tears, and hundreds of thousands, unable to make the journey, sat in their homes with bowed heads during the ceremony. Hlinka did not live to see his dream of freedom for the Slovaks fulfilled.

Dr. Szüllö and M. Esterhazy (a name well known to students of European history) are the leaders of the Hungarian minority. They also seek for equality of rights and were received by M. Hodza a few weeks ago when they put forward their claim. There seems, however, no more prospect of these claims receiving satisfaction than of similar action being taken *vis-à-vis* the other minority.

8

The Sudeten German Minority

In an article which appeared in *The American Mercury* last May, Posselt states: "The very name of the Czecho-Slovakian Republic is a lie, if by Republic is meant a free popular government in which there are no classes having exclusive privileges." The article goes on to say that: "There is no such group, ethnologically speaking, as the Czecho-Slovakian people," and "the Democratic promises made by the Republic's founders to the Allied Powers in 1919 were made in brazen fore-knowledge that they would not be kept." Two other points in this article are that: "Hundreds of thousands of persons in this Democratic nation are now faced with actual starvation" and "that 3,500,000 Sudeten Germans are doomed to extinction."

The American Mercury also published a document signed by fifty-four duly-elected representatives of the Sudeten Germans, translated into English for the first time. This document was submitted to the House of Representatives in Prague on June 1st, 1920, and to the Senate on the 9th of the same month. Part of it reads as follows:

> *"Through the Peace Treaty, a state has been created in the middle of Europe which, outside of approximately 6,500,000 Czechs, also embraces... almost 4,000,000 Germans. In vain were our protests... before the beginning of and during the peace negotiations... in vain*

we have pointed out that a state shaped like this is not in accord with Wilson's Fourteen Points, nor with the conception of democracy; that it could never find peace, and that it would represent a permanent threat to the peace of Europe.... We declare solemnly that we shall never cease to demand the self-determination of our people...."

So much for the claim made by the Czechs that the Sudeten desire for self-determination is of recent growth. *The American Mercury* proves conclusively from this and other evidence that the German protests had their birth at the time of the formation of the Czech Republic; their statement made eighteen years before the "incidents" of last May has proved a true prophecy.

"Not, of course, that all holding liberal views approve of the new Republic. In an article in The Daily Telegraph on July 25th, 1938, Mr. Lloyd George referred to it as 'the polyglot and incoherent State of Czecho-Slovakia,' and wrote of the 'incorporation in that State of hundreds of thousands of protesting Magyars and millions of angry Germans.' As he is one of the men who played a leading part at the Peace Conference his opinion is of special interest. He admits that he viewed, even in those days, Benes' 'proposed incorporation of the territory occupied by German and Magyar majorities with serious misgivings,' and that it was 'a departure from the principles laid down by the Allies during the war.' Lloyd George then requested, so he says, General Smuts to make a trip to Prague and discuss matters with President Masaryk. General Smuts 'pointed out to the President the grave undesirability of including in the Czecho-Slovak State a very large purely Magyar population living north of the Danube.... President Masaryk agreed and said he would prefer to waive all claims to the Magyar territory' - but, as Mr. Lloyd George describes in his article, Masaryk demanded 'a small strip of Hungarian territory south of the Danube' in exchange. Most of

these facts, like the treatment accorded to minorities and foreigners in Czecho-Slovakia, have remained secrets until now. But truth will out, and observers in Czecho-Slovakia are gradually sending to the outside world messages which will not fall on deaf ears.

Even British visitors are now being subjected to annoyance and even ill-treatment in this strange 'democracy.'"

9

De-Germanization

The primary preoccupation of the Czech mentality is its desire to maintain its dominant position *vis-à-vis* the other nationalities which go to form the heterogeneous State which is known as Czecho-Slovakia. It is the fervent wish of every Czech to absorb all the non-Czechs. The Czechs look upon the 3,500,000 Sudeten Germans as alien intruders in "their" country and visualize their gradual disappearance as a corporate entity. Prague has repeatedly stated its determination to expropriate German-owned land and thus to spread the Czech language to the frontiers of the new State.

Every possible means has been employed during the twenty years of the Republic's existence in the attempt to arrive at this goal. Systematic destruction of Sudeten German industry and means of livelihood has been undertaken to this end.

The economic distress now prevalent in Sudeten German areas is probably worse than in any other part of Europe. The unemployment figures have attained a record height and standards of living, low already, continue to fall. This is not the result of the world economic crisis, nor can it be traced to general trade conditions in Czecho-Slovakia. It is purely and simply the result of the Czech determination to exterminate by one means or another those Germans who are compelled to live within the marches of the Republic.

The entire State machinery is brought into play against the Sudetens. German denationalization is a Czech governmental aim and successive Czech Governments have taken pains to place Sudeten German industry at a disadvantage with its competitors. In the following pages an attempt is made to show how this policy is carried out in practice.

The country inhabited by the Sudeten Germans is thickly populated and highly industrialized. The northern half of the area contains fairly rich mineral deposits; these, in conjunction with a favourable transport situation and a supply of willing workers, have led to intensive development by those who made up some three-quarters of the whole industry of the old Dual Monarchy. Vienna and Budapest alone were industrial competitors in pre-war days. On the disruption of the Hapsburg Empire the newly-created Czecho-Slovakian State took over its most valuable industrial areas, together with Bohemia and Moravian Silesia. Manufacturing plants were chiefly in the hands of Germans. Czech industry dates from 1890 only and had attained no great importance by 1918.

It was at the express desire of the Czechs that the Sudeten German areas were included in the new State at the Peace Conference. It must be conceded that the Czech wish to possess so rich an industrial country was a natural one. Not only did the Sudeten Germans play an important part in industrial affairs, but they were also large landowners in the German-speaking area, while their financial and banking houses had an influence in the economic field commensurate with that which they erected in the field of production.

With the object of weakening German economic power the Czechs started a campaign against this key position. At the same time the policy of Czech penetration was begun, with the object of converting the purely German-speaking areas into mixed districts.

The prevalence of large estates in the Sudeten country, as opposed to the relatively small number of small holdings, has led to agitation in favour of redistribution of land, even in pre-war days. This measure of land reform, however that may be, was undertaken by the Czechs soon after the creation of the Republic. They were not, however, actuated by a zeal for social reform; their action was purely national. "Land reform" was exploited by the Czechs as a means to the expropriation of non-Slav soil, and in order to permit of the settlement of Czechs in the German-speaking districts. While the Government claimed to be taking from the rich in order to give to the poor, they made no attempt at an equitable redistribution of the confiscated acres. Over 1,250,000 acres of German land were expropriated between 1921 and 1932, with the semi-officially admitted aim of weakening the German position. This land was acquired by the State against paid or promised indemnities amounting to a mere fraction of its real value. Ninety-six per cent. of this land, all of which had been in German ownership, was allotted to Czech farmers. The German-speaking population lost one-sixth of their land and the formerly compact German enclave was now dotted with Czech cells. A negligible proportion of the land was returned to German ownership.

In the sacred name of land reform 3,250 German farmers were reduced to the state of labourers while 18,500 Czech labourers were promoted to that of farmer. The German farm labourer also suffered. According to official Czech figures there has been an increase of 66,000 in agricultural unemployment figures since this reform.

The German-owned forests were also confiscated by the State. In Bohemia alone 300,000 acres of forest land, 87% of the whole, were taken from their German owners, while the Czech forest owners in Bohemia lost only 13% of their holdings. Land reform was also used as a means to appropriate German industrial enterprises. Many German breweries, sugar factories and saw mills, shared the fate of farm and forest land. The so-called reform has been conducted in such a manner as to lead to the present-day possession by the German-speaking population of only 3% of the whole land in the Czech Republic, and has rendered acquisition of a larger proportion almost impossible.

This land appropriation was regarded by the Czechs as the most successful method of German denationalization. They adopted further means to this end: The Civil Service became predominantly Czech.

Czech nationalism was emphasized by the appearance of a horde of Czech police, customs officials, post office clerks, and the like; most of them chosen with an eye to the size of their families. They were soon followed by Czech business men and commercial travellers and attempts were made to introduce Czech working men. Wherever a Czech appeared a German lost his occupation, whether as official or labourer. In other words, he was deliberately deprived of his means of livelihood. Between 1918 and 1938 150,000 Czechs were "dumped" in German-speaking areas, giving rise to a commensurate increase in German unemployment figures.

10

De-Germanization, cont'd.

From the very first days of the new State the Czech Government started to get rid of German civil servants in order to create posts for their own nationals. Since 1918 a total of 40,000 Sudeten officials have been dismissed (cf. *The Times*, 2. 12. 37, which mentioned that tens of thousands of Germans have been dismissed in this manner).

As a result of this systematic action the proportion of posts in the administration, the postal service, railways, and other public utility concerns held by Germans is altogether incommensurate with their population ratio. In Bohemia, where 32.4% of the population is German, 29.5% postal officials were German in 1929, but this figure had fallen to 15.4% in 1930.

The percentage of Germans employed under the Ministry of Justice was 11.8%, according to a speech made by M. Hodza in November, 1937, though the German population ratio amounted to 22.4%.

From the same source we learn that there are 11% of Germans in the railway service, 13% in the revenue service, and 10% employed by the postal service.

The proportion of long-service German enlisted men is noticeably small. There are public undertakings, like the Prague post office savings bank, which employ no Germans whatsoever.

All this goes to show Czech determination to employ none but Czechs in the public service. Many Czech officials sent to German-speaking areas for the purpose of German denationalization cannot even speak the language of the district. On the other hand, on the few occasions when official posts are allotted to Germans, they are almost invariably in Czech-speaking districts. Again with the object of denationalization, more especially the case of the prospective officials' children.

The Czechs found the fact that industry was mainly in German hands intolerable. As a result, they inaugurated a policy whose aim was to weaken the German hold.

With a view to consolidation of the new State the Government inaugurated state-trading on a large scale. The object of this policy was not only the independence and security of the new Republic but envisaged also a sapping of the foundations of Sudeten German trade and industry. Czecho-Slovakia's first Foreign Minister, Dr. Stransky, described the first aim of his Government as follows:

> *"The balance of German and Czech industry in the Republic must be made equal."*

This equalization of balance was undertaken in various ways, of which two predominate. One was the creation of new industrial areas in the Czech provinces, thus cutting the throat of German industry, and the other aimed at obtaining financial control of German interests.

Sudeten German industry suffered a severe setback by the disruption of the old Dual Monarchy. While there had been 52,000,000 potential home consumers before the War only 14,000,000 were to be found in the Czech Republic. Loss of this large market led German industry to change its methods. Its leaders saw that increased exports were their only hope; they were, to some extent, successful in this up to the time of the world economic crisis.

From 1927-1929 some 60% of the entire Czech output was exported, and in the case of certain articles produced in the Sudeten areas this figure was even exceeded. By making use of the possibilities presented by foreign markets the Sudeten industrialists were able to keep going without any very great difficulty during the first decade of the Republic's existence although they received no aid from the State. With the coming of the crisis and the consequent market shrinkage, industry in the German areas began to lose ground and looked in vain for a helping hand from Prague.

They might well look in vain, for the fresh blow to Sudeten German industry was very welcome to the Czech Government whose new-born native industries were in competition with German. This new Czech industrialization must, in any event, have seriously affected German undertakings. But the Czech industries were subsidized by the State and began to turn out products which had hitherto been the sole monopoly of German industry. Thus the German firms not only lost what was left of their home markets, so necessary to them in order to finance their export trade, but had also to look on with folded hands while Czech industry supplied the needs of their own German areas.

An important factor in the situation was the placing by the Government of State orders with Czech firms exclusively; these firms were consequently able to "lower" prices as the result of Government support.

Another means employed by the Czech authorities was the methodical transfer of industry from one part of the country to another, a policy which enabled Czech capital to acquire a commanding share in Sudeten industry. Important industrial concerns in the border areas, such as the iron foundries of Rothau, were transferred inland, for no apparent or justifiable reason. These changes only meant increased suffering in German areas, for no benefit accrued to the nation as a whole by increased production.

The State Defence Act was also used by the Czechs as a pretext for the further weakening and expropriation of Sudeten German industry "for reasons of State."

This Act makes possible the forced acquisition of control in any branch of industry and allows of the removal of entire industries from frontier areas. It also permits of many other acts of interference with normal industrial procedure; it includes a remarkable clause concerning the control of workmen, which allows of the dismissal of employees without the consent of the management.

It should be emphasized that this State Defence Act, despite its name, is a purely peace-time measure. It is very loosely worded and this gives rise to fears of further action inimicable to Sudeten German industry. Professor Arnold Toynbee referred to the handicaps under which Sudeten German industry suffered by the fact of this Act, *vis-à-vis* their Czech competitors, in an article he contributed to *The Economist* in July last year, under the title of "Czecho-Slovakia's German Problem."

The influence which Czech capital has acquired in German industry within the Republic, already great, is on the increase. German businesses are compelled to deal with Czech banks and, in many cases, to borrow Czech capital from them; these banks are backed by the State. They refuse credit to firms which cannot prove that they employ a certain percentage of Czechs, all German firms being thus ineligible. Grants of credit to German firms, states Professor Toynbee, have often been made dependent on the dismissal of German workers and their replacement by Czechs.

The handicap under which German firms labour with regard to State contracts is obvious. The artificially nurtured Czech industry has been kept busy with orders from the State ever since its creation, while German tenders are systematically refused. It might reasonably have been expected that public works contracts in German-speaking areas would be awarded to German firms and German workmen. But it has always been and still is part of the German denationalization policy to allot all public contracts in the Sudeten area to Czech firms who introduce Czech labour into German areas already suffering from widespread unemployment.

Between January, 1933, and September, 1936, 540 public contracts were placed in German areas, of which 442, or 82%, went to Czech firms. Nothing has been changed in this Czech boycott of German firms, despite the solemn promise of the Prague Government following repeated representations by the Sudeten Germans, that things would be altered.

Many cases are on record where it is common knowledge that German tenders for contracts were lower than those received from Czech firms, yet in each case the contract was awarded to a Czech firm employing only Czech workmen. An example of this was published in *The Times* of December 2nd, 1937. In this case the erection of an electricity-producing plant was concerned; Czech workers from outside the area were carried to work each day by train, although the district in question was suffering from widespread unemployment.

A systematic bias is shown by the State wherever it comes into contact with Sudeten German industry. State control is on the increase, so that Prague can influence orders to a greater extent as time goes on. Production has been restricted in certain branches of industry and here again discrimination has been exercised in favour of Czech firms. The German quota of sugar production, for example, has been set at a very low figure in comparison with that for the Czechs. Restrictions on the production of margarine were introduced in 1935 and here again the dice were loaded against the German factories. New refineries near Prague in another Czech district were allowed to produce to capacity while old-established and world-renowned firms, such as Schichts of Aussig, were allotted quotas from 30%-40% below capacity, condemning a large proportion of German plant to idleness and causing the dismissal of many hands.

The Czech Government has also been using tariffs to bolster up the industry of its nationals as far as possible. Though the pleas of German industry for protective duties fell on deaf ears, high tariffs were imposed for the safeguard of Czech industry. State export subsidies are almost exclusively confined to Czech products. Interference by petty officialdom with German industry is rife. Much evidence to this effect is suppressed by the victims for fear of worse to come. A boycott of

German goods by Czechs has been quietly organized during the last months which led up to the present crisis, with the veiled approval of the Government. Sudeten industrial concerns, traders and craftsmen, all of whom depend on the home market, have been particularly hard hit. Many well-known brands produced by Sudeten firms can no longer be sold in packages bearing the imprint of their makers.

11

Unemployment

The proportion of German industrial concerns in the Republic has already been reduced by 50% through Czech economic action. The Czechs claim that the marked falling off of Sudeten industry is entirely due to the world economic crisis; this is patently untrue. It is correct to state that the Sudeten German industry suffered severely owing to the loss of foreign markets, the more so since the firms concerned were practically without reserves, but it is also true that the Prague authorities made no attempt whatever to come to their assistance. Furthermore, Czech industry has not only weathered the storm but flourished during it. The effects of the crisis on the Sudeten German firms was welcomed rather than otherwise in Czech circles, supplementing, as it did, the Governmental policy of fostering Czech industry by the award of public contracts to the exclusion of German firms.

While Sudeten unemployment was rising by leaps and bounds Czech industry prospered, a state of things still in force to-day. This applies more especially to the production of articles for immediate consumption, and also to the armament industry in which the Germans have no share whatever.

Czecho-Slovakian unemployment figures are relatively high in comparison with those of most other European countries, 643,500 workless being on the registers in March of this year, and this state of affairs is mainly due to the lamentable condition of Sudeten German industry, as is shown by the figures submitted. In March of this year there were 54 unemployed per 1,000 of the German population and only 23 per 1,000 in Czech districts.

In districts where over 80% of the population were Germans, as compared with those in which the same proportion are Czech, the German unemployment figures are 62 per 1,000, the Czech 20 per 1,000.

It is worthy of note that of the twelve districts showing the lowest unemployment figures in the whole of the Republic in March, 1938, none had a preponderantly German population, while among the twelve with the highest number of unemployed no Czech district figured. These twelve distressed areas are all German and include many thousands of acres of farm land, a fact which goes to show that this widespread unemployment is not caused, as the Czechs aver, by over-industrialization of the Sudeten areas. Further proof of this is afforded by the fact that the twelve districts with the lowest unemployment figures, all of them Czech, include two which are very highly industrial.

Since March of this year unemployment figures for the whole country have fallen slightly; this is mainly due to seasonal causes. At the end of May there were 50 unemployed per 1,000 inhabitants in mainly German-speaking districts, compared with 11 per 1,000 among the Czechs. Three years ago the Germans had only two and a half times as many unemployed as had the Czechs. The May figures speak for themselves.

The foregoing statistics are official and are taken from Prague documents. They do not give a really comprehensive report of the position, for they only include the unemployed registered at the Labour Exchanges. There are many others who have given up walking to the nearest Labour Exchange, finding it a mere waste of time.

Most countries are aware from their own experience of the terrible results of widespread unemployment. Poverty is rife; closed factories are gradually going to rack and ruin; in many cases the plant has been removed. There are no openings for the young, many of whom have never worked. Tens of thousands of families find themselves faced with a hopeless future.

The birth-rate is falling among the Sudeten Germans; to this fact the Czechs have no objection. The death-rate, on the other hand, is rising, which, again, no doubt, meets with Prague's approval.

In view of the foregoing the rise in emigration figures in the Sudeten German areas is hardly surprising. Unemployment and semi-official pressure combine to increase emigration from the mixed areas in the border districts which separate the language enclaves. Here the Czechs are particularly anxious to denationalize the non-Czechs. In 1937, 711 persons emigrated from the mixed district of Bischofteinitz, of whom 705 were Germans. As about 10,000 Germans are included in the population of 20,000 this means that every fourteenth German left his home.

While there is a constant exodus from all the German-speaking areas Czech "squatters" seldom, if ever, migrate, thus proving that there is no difficulty for a Czech to make a living in areas where German unemployment is so widespread.

It will thus be seen that the distress and poverty of the Sudeten Germans is not mainly due to economic causes, but to political and therefore removable ones. The position is due to deliberate expropriation and oppression, aimed at the accentuation of the effects of the world economic crisis on Sudeten German industry. In a letter to *The Times* on July 15th last Lord Noel-Buxton wrote of the "genuine grievance of the Germans" in Czecho-Slovakia, which, he went on, "is perhaps most easily realized if we compare Czecho-Slovakia with Ireland. If we had lost the war, and Germany had created an independent Republic in the whole of Ireland, we should, of course, have sympathized profoundly with the Northern Irish, and when we became strong enough to press the claim we should have demanded that at least autonomy be given to Ulster. Mere promises of a revision of the settlement would after twenty years, sound quite hollow.... It would have been a question of how long we were willing to wait for revision, and after twenty years we should probably have used the threat of force."

Referring to Germany, Lord Noel-Buxton added that "aggressive intention has not been proved as yet." He goes on - " The grant of adequate autonomy to the Sudeten districts is clearly indicated," and warns his readers that "the Czech Ministers may have to face the opposition of the reckless elements in the Czech electorate." He also emphasized that the Germans had "protested in 1919 against being placed under alien rule," and that "the British Labour Party strongly supported their protest" at the time. This letter was the subject of *The Times* leader on the same date. Since 1919 complaints on the part of the Sudetens have grown from year to year.

The Czech reply to all complaints by the various minorities is that the new State is still undergoing formation and change and that this cannot be accomplished without hardships. Since the new State has now been a political entity for nearly twenty years it would seem that this explanation hardly covers the facts.

12

Past the Point of No Return?

The primary preoccupation of the Prague Government is the de-nationalization of all its minorities and their absorption into the Czech whole. If they are allowed to have their way, not only the Sudeten Germans but also the Hungarians, Ruthenians and Poles will lose their individuality. Having regard to the clauses of the Treaty of St. Germain this policy on the part of the Czechs is a standing reproach to those responsible for the making of that Treaty in the name of justice and peace. In spite of all the evidence which is obvious to any competent observer the Chancelleries of Europe have as yet taken no action in the matter. It is always easiest to follow the line of least resistance, and the asseverations of Czech statesmen who boast of their regard for humanity and its rights make pleasant hearing.

The Germans who live in the bastard state of Czecho-Slovakia are made to feel that they are *persona non grata*. More and more strongly as time goes on their circumstances grow worse. They claim the rights of equal citizenship in the new Republic. It would seem that their right to political, economic, social and cultural equality can hardly, in equity, be denied. Their further demand that German-speaking territory shall no longer be regarded as a possible settlement for Czech migrants seems to be justified.

Nothing but a complete change of heart on the part of the Czechs can right the wrong done and avert a tragedy.

It is hardly surprising that the Sudeten Germans acclaim all who draw attention to their sufferings. They welcome Britons; they naturally feel thankful to Germany for various kindnesses, and their feelings were, perhaps, best described in *The Times* of August 1st, 1938, in which the report on the way they greeted Hitler at the National Gymnastic Festival at Breslau concluded as follows:

> *"Marching a few steps behind, the Sudeten German athletic leaders in turn came abreast of the tribune, received the crowd's ovation, the Führer's full salute - and broke out in isolated pairs to grasp Herr Hitler's hand. The gesture, a spontaneous variation on a protracted monotony, unloosed a rising flood of enthusiasm. The succeeding group of Sudeten German girls immediately broke their ranks, clustered round the foot of the tribune, and offered up a wild profusion of bouquets. Herr Henlein held out willing hands, and the bent-down face of the Führer broke into a smile.*
>
> *"At that point restraints were thrown aside. Marchers incontinently left their ranks, smashing down ropes and barriers, and attached themselves to the widening pyramid of arms and bodies round the Führer's tribune. The posses of Secret Service men were powerless to restore order from the growing chaos. Only the Sudeten German labour service corps, marching in an inner circle of the field, retained a vestige of discipline. Young and middle-aged Sudeten German women, their handkerchiefs to their faces, were the evident victims of fatigue and intense emotion. For an hour and a half the Badenweiler March beat out its reiterated and unheeded course. For an hour and a half the 40,000 Sudeten German athletes spent themselves in a homage such as King or President can rarely have received from the subjects of another State."*

13

The Tourist Trade

The tourist trade in Czecho-Slovakia has suffered severely in recent years. Sight-seeing tours in and around Prague are constantly abandoned owing to a lack of sight-seers. The many English and German tourists who used to frequent the country have been conspicuous by their absence lately. American visitors are almost a thing of the past.

Drastic restrictions upon foreigners are one of the main causes of this loss of the tourist trade. Passport regulations are vexatious and largely unnecessary; it is no uncommon thing for a visitor to find himself deprived of his passport for three or four days; this regulation is ostensibly directed against spies.

I, myself, was at Strbské Pleso recently. It is a pleasure resort and on the occasion of my visit was almost empty. My passport was taken from me and by reason of its absence I was unable to continue my journey. When it was returned to me I called for my bill, whereupon I was told that unless I stayed on my registration would be cancelled. It was only on my threatening to call up the British Embassy at Prague that I was permitted to leave.

A fellow guest at the hotel was without papers for three days.

As it was impossible to tell if ever one's papers would be in order, it became equally impossible to book a sleeper. When all the formalities in my case were finally completed I found that the sleeping cars were full. Had I stayed another night in this inhospitable town it would have meant fresh registration, confiscation of my passport once again, and further interminable delay. Consequently I caught the first train to Prague and, owing to the inadequacy of the rolling stock, stood for most of the ten-hour journey.

The British are not welcomed outside Prague. On my return from any excursion into the surrounding country my car was invariably searched for contraband. On one three-hour drive from Prague to Marienbad my passport was minutely examined no less than three times.

Hotel proprietors in German and Slovak territory are friendly enough and sincerely regret the present state of affairs, but the law is there and they have to obey it.

Vexatious inquisition which the law renders obligatory at every hotel, renders travelling a thing to avoid. Tourists who are used to the hospitable treatment they receive in most civilized European countries generally leave Czecho-Slovakia after the shortest of stays, much to the astonishment of the Czechs, who regard their much-vaunted Republic as an earthly paradise.

The Slovaks deny their kinship with the Czechs. Their Travel Propaganda Bureaux advertise "Slovakia" without the "Czecho" (posters such as "Visit the Slovakian Paradise" may often be seen). One meets with a friendly welcome in Slovakia but this is spoilt by the petty persecution of Czech officials. The Czech mentality is only happy when annoying and harassing others. On the few occasions when they tire of ill-treating the minorities they turn their attention to tourists, as a relaxation.

The country is in a state of constant unrest. Street fights are a daily occurrence in Prague; during the municipal elections clashes between parties took place in all districts. The police are armed *cap à pie* with truncheons, swords and automatics - the visitor has the impression of being in a war zone.

I was present recently when a street fight occurred in Prague. - Turning a corner I came upon some 2,000 Czechs gathered together in front of the German House where the Sudeten Germans were holding a meeting. When the proceedings finished and the Germans tried to leave the dense crowd of Czechs refused to make way. On the arrival of the police the Germans were advised to leave in groups of twos and threes by a side door. This naturally took a long time and those who were impatient for their beds finally decided to leave in a body. They were roughly handled by the crowd and fighting became general, amid hysterical cries from the Czechs. Whether by design or not the small force of Czech police was quite inadequate to control the crowd.

These continual disorders and the general lack of discipline among the officials contribute to driving tourists from the country. Systematic overcharging of foreigners is widespread. It is advisable for the foreign visitor to keep a sharp eye on taxi drivers, who are in the habit of tampering with their meters unless closely watched.

Democracy as we know it does not exist in Czecho-Slovakia. The country is plagued with a horde of officials and bureaucrats and is ruled by force alone.

Conscription in Czecho-Slovakia is more widely applied than in any other country in the world. At the time of the "incidents" in May last, boys of sixteen were called to the colours. They were provided with arms and equipment, but no uniforms, and marched about the country in undisciplined bands, a danger to themselves and others. Railway lines were everywhere guarded by men in mufti bristling with weapons. Motor cars were seized and foreign motorists were constantly held up and searched. In more than one case seats and upholstery were ripped up in a search for "incriminating documents."

Even when the crisis was over soldiers with fixed bayonets were still to be seen on the platforms of railway stations; even the main line stations of Prague - the Wilson and the Masaryk depots - were no exception.

"Hiking" in mountain and forest land should only be undertaken at one's own risk, for Czech outposts are dotted about all over the place and one is constantly stumbling on sentries with fixed bayonets. In Slovakia and the Sudeten German areas there is intense bitterness against the troops, who trample crops and make a general nuisance of themselves to the farmers. The Czech soldiery largely consists of raw recruits without discipline and inadequately supplied with reliable N.C.O's.

The Jews, who are accorded special unofficial privileges, seem to be the only people who find conditions in Czecho-Slovakia tolerable and even customary.

The official Czech Travel Bureaux have scarcely any work for their employees and guides. Nevertheless Prague manages to exist comfortably enough at the expense of the minorities.

Plans are on foot to prevent any foreigner earning a living in the Republic. No English is taught in the schools. German is more or less a *lingua franca,* but those who speak it are looked on with suspicion by the Czechs. The permission given by the English Government to Henlein to visit London was regarded by the Czechs as an unfriendly act. They are obsessed with the idea that England and France should assist them in keeping down their non-Czech population. A sense of justice does not enter into their composition, nor have they the faintest idea of the workings of a true democracy.

The Czechs are prospering, as has already been pointed out, for the moment, at the expense of the minorities. This is a state of affairs which can hardly continue, for business is becoming harder and harder to carry on under the twin handicaps of state interference and constant disorders.

It is not the English habit to look with favour upon deserters. Many Czechs have proudly described to me how they crossed to the enemy lines during the War. They have never regarded themselves as traitors, for they hold that in pre-war days they were an oppressed people living against their will under an alien government and were thus entitled to fight for their own freedom. When I suggested that the position of the various minorities, within their own frontiers, was exactly analogous to their own in pre-war days they said that that was " quite different," though they were unable to adduce any argument in favour of that difference.

They trust no race other than their own and distrust more especially the racial minorities within their gates. This is hardly surprising for, having once stabbed in the back the country of which they formed part, they are now constantly on the lookout for similar conduct on the part of those they are oppressing.

14

Feasibility of Autonomous Minority States

England has been mainly instrumental in securing the independence of Lithuania, Latvia and Esthonia. Separate states were created in each case, the inhabitants of which, though closely related, are not of identical race. There is a far greater difference between the various peoples who inhabit Czecho-Slovakia.

While there can be no doubt of Czech terrorism, retaliation to it has wisely been held in check by the various minority leaders. In a leading article on May 23rd last, *The Times* referred to the shooting of Sudeten Germans in the following words:

> *"The most serious incident was the shooting of two Sudeten Germans by a Czech policeman.... It is satisfactory and reassuring to note that this act of violence - whether justified or not - did not produce any impetuous counter-action.... In their own particular regions German minority form the bulk of the population... the minorities - and not only the Sudeten Germans - are being promised self-administration and proportionate representation in the control of public business...."*

Again, from *The Times* of July 15th:

"It is common ground that the condition of the Sudeten ought to have been improved many years ago."

That goes to the root of the distrust of the Prague Government felt by all the minorities. Prague has been lavish with promises during the last twenty years, but has done no single act to implement them. The Nationalities Statute which might have put a stop to racial quarrels if brought into force eighteen years ago, is now being held out as a future prospect. To the minorities' demand for autonomy the Czechs counter that this would be to create "states within a state" and that this would lead to a state of affairs rendering central government impossible. When faced with the existence not only of Switzerland but also of the British Commonwealth of free Nations the Czechs have no reply.

Formation of an autonomous Czech State has more ethnographical and geographical justification than had any of the Baltic countries. The same remarks apply to Sudeten Germany and Ruthenia.

There are a number of countries in Europe whose populations are smaller than those of any of the provinces mentioned. Were the Czech State to be deprived of its racial minorities it would still be a considerable power with a population of 7,500,000. It has never been suggested that Greece, with a population of 6,200,000, is too small to continue to exist. Sweden has 6,000,000 inhabitants, a population considerably below that of Greater London, and manages to exist very comfortably. Denmark, a country where poverty is almost unknown, is a state with 3,750,000 inhabitants. Finland has but 3,000,000. The Sudetens - 3,500,000 strong - exceed in population Finland, Norway, the Irish Free State, Lithuania, Latvia, Esthonia, Albania, and Luxemburg. It will thus be seen that a Sudeten State would be by no means the smallest in Europe. As a *reductio ad absurdum* one might point to the continued existence of Monaco, San Marino and Andorra. Further, if we take overseas examples, there is New Zealand, a flourishing pastoral country with a rapidly expanding industry and but 1,600,000 inhabitants.

There can be no doubt that Czechs, Sudetens, Slovaks, and Ruthenians are sufficiently numerous to form a state each. Political economy appears to raise no objection to such an action. Nor is the claim that Czechs and Slovaks are one people tenable. There are much greater differences between the Czechs and Slovaks than there are between Latvians and Lithuanians. The Czech language is distinct from the Slovak, though both have a common root. Customs and ways of life differ widely between the two countries.

Having regard to these national differences it can hardly be denied that the Slovaks are entitled to a State of their own. It seems unfortunate that England, so largely instrumental in obtaining the grant of independence to Esthonia, Latvia, Lithuania, cannot be persuaded to do the same thing for Slovaks, Sudetens and Ukrainians.

Czechs themselves would benefit by the action desired by their minorities, for they would cease to be in the position of ruling a hybrid State, 50% of whose population is passively, if not actively, disloyal to the Central Government.

It is of course true that there would still exist minorities even in a new State. In a new Sudeten State, with a population of 3,500,000 or thereabouts, there would be about 300,000 Czechs; Slovakia would contain 100,000 Czechs and an almost equal number of Germans. That is unavoidable, such small groups would have to make the best of the situation or, it might be possible, to proceed to an exchange of population such as was successfully accomplished between Greece and Turkey.

The frontier problem is simple enough of solution. There are no natural boundaries between Latvia and Lithuania, nor between either of those two States and Poland. Yet those frontiers are respected, drawn as they were along ethnographical lines.

What has been done on the shores of the Baltic can be repeated in Central Europe. Lithuania, Poland, Esthonia and Latvia each had a minorities problem, which each has successfully solved. It should be the duty of all the Democracies to ensure a similar solution in Czecho-Slovakia. Slovaks and Sudetens are as much entitled to self-determination as

Lithuanians or Latvians. They would be up in arms immediately if any one of the Baltic States endeavoured to swallow its neighbours under cover of a smoke screen of a new State with a high-sounding hybrid title. Can the Democracies, then, continue their complacent acceptance of a state of affairs where one-half of the Czecho-Slovakian population holds down the other half by brute force?

15

A Solution to the Minority Problem

Though, to a certain extent, one can understand and appreciate Czech ambitions tending towards the aggrandisement of their country, yet the fulfilment of such ambitions must not be at the expense of the birthright of incorporated nationalities. In addition to the formation of the national states we have already contemplated, justice demands that the 800,000 Hungarians who are at present cut off by artificial boundaries should be returned to their own country. The northern bank of the Danube from Pressburg to Budapest always has been Hungarian soil and should become so once more. The two areas form in reality one economic unit. Much economic distress has been caused by their enforced separation.

On the other hand, justice could not be satisfied by the allocation of Slovakia to Hungary, for Hungary oppressed Slovakia in the past and racial enmity still subsists. It would be anomalous to free the Slovaks from the yoke of Prague only to hand them over to Budapest; to give them one form of servitude in exchange for another would be a travesty of justice.

That justice demands that Slovakia be an independent State having its own government with definitely stipulated and firmly founded rights opposite Prague. The Slovaks do not want to be controlled either by Czechs, Germans, or Hungarians.

As regards the Poles, the best solution is to give them back to their own country. They live in the Tatra district on the Galician frontier so that this solution would present no difficulties. The country has few natural resources and its soil is very poor. The population is down-trodden and poverty-stricken and is in dire need of the aid which could be afforded to it by its Polish fellow countrymen. Geographically the mountains should be Polish.

The Sudeten Germans are equally entitled to benefit by the principle of self-determination. It is time and high time that they were free from their thraldom to Prague. They are racially very different from all their neighbours in the Czech Republic. It must not be forgotten that it has taken twenty years to induce the Czechs to go even so far as drafting the Nationality Statute. It might well be a further twenty years before they can bring themselves to put it into effect. If President Benes, who is as stubborn as ever his French counterpart "Poincaré la Guerre," had his way it will never be put into effect. President Benes is a man of simple origin whose tastes have remained as spartan as his upbringing. His mind is non-receptive to new ideas and he is totally unable to appreciate the point of view of those who differ from him. To this one-track mind a general European war is preferable to any diminution of the Czech realm. Unlike M. Poincaré he covers the iron hand with a velvet glove. He expresses his sympathy with the minorities but refuses to make any practical attempt to give satisfaction to their complaints. He is a Czech Imperialist who simply cannot understand that any citizen of the Czech Republic should have ambitions other than for that Republic. Benes is the real stumbling block in the way of the Nationality Statute.

It seems probable that Hodza would have been willing to make concessions years ago. His knowledge of the minorities question is deep and his views are sympathetic to the minorities. But he is not so strong a man as Benes, whose tactics are gradually wearing him down. Had he been President, or were he even free to act now, he might and probably would have found a peaceful solution to the problem. Under Benes' autocratic rule his hands are tied.

A Czech intention of shelving the problem has been openly stated in the National Press. *Hranicar,* for example, says:

> *"...Let no one interfere in our domestic affairs. It is our states-manlike duty to persuade England that the forebearance which she urges us to exercise in the interests of the Nazi Party, is in reality doing disservice to England herself."*

The *Neue Züricher Zeitung* expresses grave doubts as to Czech intentions. The opinion of this Swiss paper is the more valuable since it is opposed to National Socialism and its circulation is, in fact, prohibited in the Reich.

On June 30th last this paper had a leader from which the following is an extract:

> *"Has President Benes, who is said to be determined to defend the unity of Czecho-Slovakia in a new battle in the Weisser Berg, sufficient authority to persuade the Czech Nationalists, Hussite standard bearers, to have some understanding of German interests? Has the Prime Minister, whose whole career proves his expert understanding of the minorities problem, sufficient diplomatic skill to make the National Czech Coalition toe the line?"*

The paper puts the matter in a nutshell. Hodza has already resigned and so shown his inability on this point so that as a result the fate of Europe is actually dependent on the actions of the indomitable Dr. Benes. Parliament is powerless; the Democratic machine exists only on paper.

The Daily Herald is also numbered among those who have come to realize the ill-treatment suffered by the Sudeten Germans. Its Special Correspondent, Mr. Ewer, recently paid a visit to the Sudeten areas and his dispatches proved the truth of the allegations concerning closed factories and "Czech" dumping. As the *Herald* is notoriously a Germanophobe organ, Germany's worst enemy could hardly accuse it of being under Nazi control. The evidence given in its columns is the most conclusive proof that anyone could wish for that even the friends of Prague and the enemies of Berlin are being compelled by the sheer weight of facts to admit that there is something amiss in the Republic of Czecho-Slovakia.

The discussions now at last in progress were impeded by the Czech nationals in every possible manner and drastic measures were taken further to depress the condition of the minorities. The Spiro paper mills were moved at the very last moment from Böhmisch-Kramau to Prague. As this firm was the only considerable one in the former town the move means increased unemployment. Even while Lord Runciman was packing prior to his trip to Prague the Managing Director of a sugar refinery in Aussig announced his intention of moving the whole concern to Prague.

The ruin of the minorities and especially of the Sudeten minority was hastened although elsewhere efforts which promised to be satisfactory, were being made to bring about a just settlement.

But the Czech corps of officers have already stated that they are determined to oppose any development along the suggested lines. The Declaration published last month in the Army weekly, *Dustoynicke Listy,* which was tantamount to a demand for a rebellion against the Hodza Government, proves this. The officers in the Czech Army are almost exclusively of Czech nationality; they stated "that they would not permit" the overstepping of certain limits. Their Manifesto can hardly be regarded as a friendly gesture at the moment of Lord Runciman's arrival in Prague as an impartial mediator. Paris was filled with rumours as to the possibility of a military dictatorship overthrowing Hodza's Government consequent on the publication of this Manifesto. The Czech officers had much the same position in relation to the civil population as had those of Germany in pre-war days. They have no intention of renouncing their various privileges and will doubtless keep on to the very end with their sabotage of all efforts at appeasement.

Henlein is reported by *The Daily Telegraph* on July 26th last as saying:

> *"I will never ask my people to accept mere promissory phrases. This time there will have to be a real agreement based on genuine concessions by the other side as well as by our own."*

There was, however, from the very start but little likelihood of any such concessions being granted. Lord Runciman was unable to get his way with the stubborn Benes. The Czech President has an iron will and the usual selfish obstinacy of the die-hard temperament. Many in this country are prone to think that British interests necessarily coincide with those of Czecho-Slovakia. This is not so. Again to quote *The Times* (25. 7. 38), Wiedemann, Hitler's A.D.C., stated that: "There were no fundamental differences that need separate the British and German peoples. Everything was capable of arrangement." In the same issue *The Times* added: "Herr Hitler sent an assurance that the German Government were anxious for a peaceful solution of the Sudeten German problem." *The Daily Telegraph* (21. 7. 38) remarks: "The Foreign Secretary expressed gratification at the spirit of Herr Hitler's message."

There is one way to achieve a satisfactory solution of the Czech problem, namely, by a secret plebiscite under English and, therefore, impartial supervision. In this manner England would be upholding the cause of world peace, a cause which cannot but suffer by threats employed by any nation against any other.

That Great Britain is the country most suitable to perform this task is clear. *The Daily Telegraph* (27. 7. 38) confirms this, adding that Herr Kundt, Henlein's second in command, "welcomes the mission of Viscount Runciman and states that the Sudeten German Party will afford him every assistance."

Germany appears to have had the same opinion, for on July 26th last, the *Angriff* stated: "The British observer may count on Germany's best wishes in his difficult and delicate mission." In other words it was the universal opinion that England was the one country who could have conducted a plebiscite to the satisfaction of all interested parties.

The plebiscite would, of course, have had to be carried out in accordance with strictly Democratic principles - on the lines, say, of a General Election in England. The questions asked would have had to be clear and simple, for instance, "Are you a Czech?", "Are you a German?", "Are you a Slovak?", and so on. Consequent on this secret census the various peoples of Czecho-Slovakia would have had to be given self-government or transferred to the countries to which they really belong. The Swiss system is not really suitable to the present case, for while Switzerland has a centuries-old tradition, Czecho-Slovakia has nothing of the sort. Meanwhile, this possibility has been ruled out by the course of events. On the whole, the national groups will obtain their independence even without plebiscites. At the moment of writing, however, it is difficult to foretell how it will plan out, to which side they will lean, whether they will become completely independent States or live side by side with the Czechs in a Federal Community. It would, for instance, be feasible for the Sudeten areas to form an autonomous State. With upwards of four million inhabitants this Sudeten State would be quite big enough to stand on its own feet. More probably, however, such a Sudeten State would of its own volition soon cease to be independent and become part of Greater Germany. Incidentally, this would be the most natural thing in the world. In the case of the Poles and the Hungarians the situation is similar. Here, too, it would be only natural if without much ado and formalities they would be permitted to return to their respective countries. The purely Czech areas with 7,500,000 inhabitants, Slovakia with 2,500,000 and, finally, Carpatho-Ukraine could then form a Confederation of autonomous States, each having jurisdiction over its own affairs and co-operating only with regard to representation abroad and finances according to well-considered and definite lines. The Slovaks and Carpatho-Ukrainians would surely welcome such a solution which conforms with self-determination. I even believe if the Czechs themselves were asked instead of President Benes and his minions in Prague there would be no opposition. The Czech question would thus be finished forever and a day, and European fears as to the future of peace would be allayed.

It has often been said that there is no need for England to have to act as "world policeman." That may be so. But England has been responsible for the creation of many of the smaller European States, and, through Mr. Lloyd George, took a large share in the creation of the Czech Republic, although the Czechs gave the credit for it to President Wilson. On this account she cannot evade her share of responsibility for the present situation.

England alone with her age-long tradition for fair play and justice can take the initiative for all. Speaking of the difficulties of his position Lord Runciman described himself as a small boat alone on the wastes of the Atlantic. Prague made no secret of its hostility to his mission. The official Czech Press Bureau stated: "We will keep an anxious watch on our vital interests, independence and control of our own internal affairs," a statement implying that Lord Runciman should take care to avoid any appearance of action. Nevertheless, it is clearly England's duty to stand by those whose national status was guaranteed by the terms of the Peace Treaty, and whose wrongs under Czech rule are now patent to all. There can be only one solution to the problem - the right of self-determination for those who are unwilling any longer to endure the "benevolent" rule of President Benes. England should live up to her reputation for fairness, which would only be in keeping with the anxiety expressed by *The Daily Telegraph* on July 28th that "nothing should be left undone which might help to heal one of the sore spots in Central Europe liable to inflammation if not properly treated.".

That England is the only country able to undertake the task of doing something, was borne out by the speech made by Mr. Chamberlain at a dinner in Birmingham on July 14th, 1938, when he said:

"I am thoroughly convinced that the influence that this country can exert for good or evil - for others as well as for ourselves - is more powerful than that of any other country in the world. This is partly due to our inherent strength and to the many resources of which we are possessed. But it is due also to a general, if not universal, recognition of the fact that our policy as a country is not directed merely by selfish interest, but that it is rooted in the conviction that there can be no peace or security or permanency of happiness for mankind except under the rule of law and order, of reason, and of good faith.

"It is much easier to formulate maxims of this kind than it is to apply them in practice, and those who endeavour to steer by these general but deep-seated principles should expect to suffer many disappointments and set-backs. They have their motives misrepresented and their sincerity doubted. But men who are worthy of their salt are not going to be turned from their purpose by temporary inconveniences or annoyances of that kind. The Government of which I am at present the head intends to hold on its course, which is set for the appeasement of the world.

"We know that in every country there are vast multitudes of men and women who pray daily and nightly for the success of our efforts. We believe that by the example that we set to others that we can eventually win through to our goal, and when the time comes for us to hand on our responsibilities to others we shall be able to leave behind us a calmer and a safer world."

The whole British public wishes to assist in a solution - and could do so. *The Times* remarked in a leader on June 3rd, 1938, that:

"...the letters which continue to reach this office bear witness to the interest taken in its (Czecho-Slovakia's) solution by British public opinion. One which was published yesterday from the Dean

of St. Paul's was typical of many, and an effective expression of the view that the Germans of Czecho-Slovakia ought to be allowed, by plebiscite or otherwise, to decide their own future - even if it should mean their secession from Czecho-Slovakia to the Reich. With this view the majority of Englishmen probably agree..."

Further to the foregoing it seems only fair - within the accepted rights of self-determination - that the Sudetens should have the option of deciding whether they will become an independent State or whether they prefer inclusion in the Reich. In either case, an exchange of German and Czech populations could be arranged under the supervision of a British Commission.

In a letter to *The Times* (2. 6. 38), Mr. W. R. Matthews supposes "that the British Empire has now adopted the view that it is both wrong and unwise to coerce a people into remaining within a state system against their will." He also referred to the possibility of the Sudetens wishing to join Germans with the following words:

> *"I take it to be evident that the overwhelming majority of the Sudeten Germans wish to be incorporated in the Reich and that geography does not forbid this. I want to know on what moral grounds could we base a refusal to support a plebiscite to determine the future of these people.*
>
> *"It might, I suppose, be said that they do not know what is best for them, or that they have been carried away by propaganda, or that they hold a most unreasonable political theory - in short, all the common arguments against democracy might be used. Or, again, it might be said that their separation from Czecho-Slovakia would weaken that country and disturb the balance of power. I do not see how this could be urged with any show of reason, because it is difficult to think that the inclusion of several million people who are opposed to the State of which they are nominal members can be anything but a source of weakness."*

The letter concluded with the words:

"It would indeed be a tragic irony if, having fought one war, as we are assured, for the principle of self-determination, we found ourselves involved in another to prevent its application."

The present position is untenable; immediate action is required. Things are becoming more complicated every day and the longer decisive action is deferred the more difficult the problem will become, and the greater will be the danger to the peace of Europe, which - when all is said and done - is surely the main consideration.

As regards the plebiscite, its results would have to be accepted by all concerned; that is to say, in the events of Sudetens, Hungarians, Poles or others voting in favour of union with their brothers, Prague would have to agree. On the other hand, any group which preferred the *status quo* would have to understand that it would become a part of the polyglot Republic once and for all. It seems unlikely that this would happen, but all contingencies would have to be provided for, and the result of the plebiscite made binding on all interested parties - that is to say, Germany, Poland and Hungary, as well as the national minorities. Preparatory to the holding of a plebiscite all Czech troops, police and secret service agents would have to be withdrawn from the areas described in official Czech publications as mainly German, Polish or Hungarian. Only then could British officials carry out a plebiscite in the knowledge that no pressure was being exerted on the various populations. Special local police could then be enlisted from the local population.

It would seem as though the immediate adoption of some such proposals as were made by Kundt (see Appendix A) can prevent further bloodshed in the Republic and so avoid European complications. The time to act is *now*, not next year or the year after. The eleventh hour has struck and any further procrastination may well be fatal.

Prominent personages in France see no objection to the solution heretofore proposed. In *Le Revue de France* of August 1st this year, on page 295, President Flandin's views on possible German expansion are given. He states quite definitely that France and England should seek a basis for an *entente* with Germany and is of the opinion that German expansion would not affect France's vital interests. His words are:

> *"Would Germany's economic expansion in Central and Eastern Europe along the Danube, always provided that the territorial independence of the States bordering on that river is respected, be of a nature seriously to affect France's major interest.*
>
> *"Whilst France is a great Continental Power she is, at the same time, a great Colonial Power, with possessions in all quarters of the globe, which would be the most dangerous for us: to see Germany expanding in Central Europe or, on the contrary, spreading all over the globe, notably in Mediterranean regions, and seeking to wrest from us and from our English friends various of our imperial possessions?*
>
> *"Of two evils we have to choose the lesser. For my part, my choice is made. In the solution of this question France and England are bound by common interests and aspirations. It is obviously our duty to seek for the basis of an accord with Germany in agreement with, and by common action with, Great Britain."*

The neutrality of the new States whose creation is envisaged, that is to say, the lesser Czech Republic, Slovakia and Ruthenia, would have to be the object of a guarantee by the Great Powers acting in concert, supplementing the nonaggression pact signed by the neighbour States.

A condition inseparable from this guarantee would be that the three new States should bind themselves to a strict neutrality and no longer act as advance landing grounds for the U.S.S.R. It can hardly cause surprise that Germany should be strenuously opposed to any form of alliance between Prague and Moscow. It is certainly not to England's advantage to give the Soviets new footholds in Europe, as has been amply proved by the Spanish Civil War.

England can arrange all this if she wishes. *The Times* (4. 8. 38) referred to the tribute paid to her by M. André Thérive who recently wrote in *Figaro:* "England proves by her example what civilization really is. Instead of ceaselessly seeking for the theory of it she is content to practise it." *The Times* concluded its leading article that day with the words:

> *"Mutatis mutandis the foreign policy of this country is to try to play its part with honour in defence of its own interests, but always with due regard for the legitimate claims of others, and by fair dealing to establish relations of confidence and concord with an ever-widening circle of States. The one principle that is always valid is to act justly on every issue as it arises."*

This paragraph aptly describes England's position. It is now for her to apply her usual fair-mindedness to the legitimate aims of the Czecho-Slovakian minorities, and to extend to them the benefits of the principle of self-determination. A wrong which was done in 1919 can, to-day, be righted. It is never too late to right a wrong, and the fleeting opportunity that is afforded at the present moment should be grasped with resolution and whole-hearted decision.

16

Facsimile Appendix

Scans of pages 93-126 of the original 1938 book.

Tables

TABLE I

The trend of Development of the German Population in N.W. Bohemia.

The percentage of Germans among the whole population (excluding foreigners) was as follows :

Circuit	In 1921	In 1930	Circuit	In 1921	In 1930
Brüx .	. 52.8	50.9	Lobositz .	. 54.2	50.3
Oberleutendorf	. 62.3	63.1	Katharinaberg	. 99.3	98.4
Dux . .	. 57.7	57.4	Sebastiansberg	. 99.4	97.7
Bilin .	. 65.7	61.4	Görkau .	. 87.5	82.8
Teplitz-Schönau .	76.7	75.3	Komotau .	. 92.4	87.4
Karbitz .	. 80.4	78.6	Kaaden .	. 96.0	94.0
Aussig .	. 83.1	80.0	Postelberg	. 60.6	57.1
Tetschen .	. 93.7	89.8	Saaz .	. 87.0	79.5
Leitmeritz .	. 62.6	57.4	Podersam .	. 90.0	83.3

TABLE II

The percentage of Czechs was as follows :

Circuit	In 1921	In 1930	Circuit	In 1921	In 1930
Tetschen .	. 5.13	8.09	Leitmeritz .	. 32.09	35.50
Dauba .	. 12.13	17.04	Rumburg .	. 2.26	4.38
Deutsch-Gabel .	2.75	5.77	Schluckenau	. 2.47	3.92
Böhmisch-Leipa .	7.69	12.03	Aussig .	. 17.36	20.04
Gratzau .	. 8.62	10.06	Warnsdorf .	. 5.57	7.18

TABLE III

Results of the first stage of the local government elections in large towns.

Town	Votes recorded	German Total	German S.D.P.	Soc. Dem.	Czech	Communist	German percentage
Aussig .	29,303	22,956	19,874	3,082	4,473	1,338	78
Tetschen .	8,848	7,375	6,704	671	1,473	—	83
Böhm. Leipa	9,066	6,708	6,274	434	1,996	389	74
Brüx .	17,318	11,243	10,671	572	5,385	716	65
Dux .	8,381	4,209	3,669	540	3,459	713	over 50
Sternberg .	8,397	7,543	6,266	1,277	707	148	abt. 90
Neutitschein	9,007	6,456	5,725	731	2,431	120	,, 72

TABLE IV

Town	Votes recorded	German Total	German S.D.P.	Soc. Dem.	Czech	Communist	German percentage
Gablonz .	23,141	19,143	18,577	566	3,193	805	80
Komotau .	22,622	18,990	17,018	1,972	2,663	969	almost 94

TABLE V

District	Votes recorded	German Total	S.D.P.	Soc. Dem.	Czech	Communist	German percentage
Bilin	6,811	4,047	3,718	329	2,373	391	60
Bruch nr. Brüx	5,290	1,906	1,465	421	1,897	1,487	36
Ladowitz nr. Dux	3,087	1,351	1,033	318	1,079	657	abt. 44
Nestomitz nr. Aussig	2,396	1,400	1,174	226	682	314	„ 60
Probstau nr. Teplitz	2,485	1,476	1,122	354	879	130	„ 60
Prödlitz nr. Aussig	3,224	1,889	1,499	389	719	617	„ 59
Seestadt	3,046	1,636	1,392	241	1,237	176	„ 54
Tannwald	2,962	1,702	1,634	68	975	285	„ 60

On the other hand, we have the following :

Town	Votes recorded	German Total	S.D.P.	Soc. Dem.	Czech	Communist	German percentage
Freiwaldau	4,803	4,432	4,302	130	302	69	abt. 92
Georgswalde	5,068	4,703	4,612	91	179	186	„ 93
Osset	5,896	3,940	3,539	401	1,316	440	„ 67

TABLE VI

Town	Votes recorded	German Total	S.D.P.	Soc. Dem.	Czech	Communist	German percentage
Reichenberg	25,559	20,872	19,766	1,106	3,788	899	abt. 82
Teplitz-Schönau	20,535	15,340	13,932	1,408	3,161	644	„ 75
Troppau	19,713	14,762	13,835	927	4,741	210	„ 75
Warnsdorf	15,000	13,053	11,553	1,500	827	1,120	„ 87
Bodenbach	15,055	12,742	10,133	2,609	2,012	301	„ 84
Saaz	12,157	9,981	9,040	941	1,812	364	„ 82
Iglau	20,419	7,670	7,418	252	11,955	894	„ 33
Graslitz	8,993	8,532	7,554	978	250	211	„ 92
Schönberg	9,718	8,432	7,940	492	1,228	58	„ 86
Trautenau	10,132	7,971	7,263	708	2,065	96	„ 78
Leitmeritz	11,281	7,654	7,394	260	3,401	226	„ 68

(N.B.—There were 1,390 Jewish votes among the Communist poll at Teplitz-Schönau).

TABLE A

Nationality	Pressburg			Kashau			Uzhorod		
	1910	1921	1930	1910	1921	1930	1910	1921	1930
Hun-garians	31,705	20,731	18,890	33,350	11,206	11,504	13,590	7,712	4,499
Germans	32,790	25,837	32,801	3,189	2,145	3,354	1,151	433	508
Czecho-Slovaks	11,674	37,038	60,013	6,548	31,572	42,245	1,209	5,064	8,030
Jews ..	—	3,758	4,747	—	5,275	5,733	—	3,743	5,897
Ruthenians	—	—	—	—	—	—	641	2,807	6,260
Totals	76,169	87,364	116,451	43,087	50,198	62,836	16,591	19,759	25,194

TABLE B

Percentage of Hungarians among inhabitants.

Place	Per-centage	Place	Per-centage	Place	Per-centage	Per-centage
Tornalja	. 83.1	Szepsi .	. 56.3	Kassa . 12.6		
Feled .	. 77.4	Vagsellye	. 55.5	Rimaszom-bat . 13.2		
Dunaszerdahely 88.2		Rozsnyo	. 35.1	Pressburg . 13.0		
Parkany	. 81.6	Leva .	. 27.8	(Pozsony)		
Zseliz .	. 79.4	Ersekujvar	. 31.6	Towns		
Komarom .	82.9	. Ungvar	. 26.7	(in 1,000)		
Kiralyhelmec .	77.7	Verebely	. 25.7	Komarom	12.65	63.6
Somorja .	76.9	Kekko .	. 27.0	Leva .	4.97	41.0
Ipolysag .	72.8	Losono	. 25.8	Losono .	4.00	27.5
Bergszasz .	71.5	Munkacs	. 18.0	Rozsnvo	3.21	50.7
Galanta .	62.0	Nyitra	. 13.8	Rimaszom-bat .	3.50	48.0

TABLE C

District	1921 Czech population in percentage	1923 Czech votes in percentage
Lutynia Niemiecka . . .	79.5	51.6
Strzeczon . . .	53.5	43.3
Wierzniowice . . .	65.6	45.1
Darkow	31.7	13.9
Olbrachcice . . .	31.7	11 1
Raj	19.0	5.5
Stonawa	41.4	7 2
Sucha Gorna . . .	30.4	16.8
Stanislowice . . .	67.7	41.6
Grodziszcze . . .	50.0	24.2
Cierlik Gorny . . .	56.4	29.3
Cierlik Dolny . . .	65.5	33.0
Zukow Gorny . . .	74.8	19.8

TABLE D

The Czech population and Votes in 1930.

District				Census percentage	Local Government Elections percentage
Lutynia Niemiecka	.	.	.	83.7	48.2
Strzeczon	.	.	.	62.3	41.9
Darkow .	.	.	.	48.0	29.5
Marklowice	.	.	.	54.7	36.6
Lutynia Polska .	.	.	.	77.6	47.3
Zukow Dolny .	.	.	.	35.6	16.0

Appendix A

Only Alterations in the Form of State to be Considered.

STATEMENTS made by Herr Kundt, member of the Prague Parliament, to Premier Hodza on August 18th, 1938.

The following quotations from *Die Zeit* of August 18th, 1938, show that the Sudeten Germans are no longer willing to accept half measures. The report ran as follows :

" The statement of the Premier that our proposals and the Government drafts are a suitable basis, not only formally, but also actually, for the negotiations is in contrast to the rejecting attitude of the Government and the Coalition Committees. The Government drafts are actually diametrically opposed to the contents of our own draft, and to our conception of the solution to the Nationalities problem. It is, therefore, all the more important, if an agreement is sought, not to discuss partial questions and not to run through the Government draft one paragraph at a time, but to discuss the different points of view, and to see whether and how a common point of view can be reached, from which the partial questions can be arranged.

" Although the results of our discussion with the Government and the present view of the Government and the Sudeten German Party are still separated by the same gap as before, we are still prepared to negotiate as to how practical alterations in the form of the State, the creation of corresponding conditions, and other similar measures can lead to the solution of the Nationalities problem, and thus of the State crisis on the basis of the eight points demanded by Konrad Henlein at Karlsbad. We wish to point out to you, however, that the patience of our population, who have not as yet seen any sign of goodwill on your part, is not so great as our own. You need not be

97

surprised that Sudeten Germans are driven to feel increasingly great distrust towards you so long as Czech organizations and personages, as well as Government newspapers, show no sign of goodwill, but vie with each other in their attacks on Sudeten Germans and the German people as a whole.

" It is dangerous, moreover, that the Association of Czecho-Slovakian officers has issued the well-known proclamation, which is diametrically opposed to the assurances of the Government, as well as to the assurances you recently gave. How can the German population believe the assurances of the Government when such a proclamation as that of the officers can appear without being officially disavowed by the Government ? Our negotiations can only be continued when not only the statements made at the round table, but also the attitude of the Czech Press, the Czech organizations, and State officials, as well as corresponding measures to create psychological essentials on the part of the Government and the supporting Czech Government parties prove the announced goodwill to the public.

" We have not overlooked the repeated emphasis of goodwill on the part of the Premier, and, at the last discussion, also on the part of his colleagues, Meissner, Klapka and Ostrey. But the decisive point is whether this goodwill is really there. For the rest, we return the expressions of goodwill, in the expectation that you, too, will believe in our goodwill, which we have proved despite all the experiences of heretofore. But I must remark that your Press has not acknowledged our good and honest intentions up to now.

" Unfortunately, I find that the drafts placed before us are in no way other than those expressed in your original statement, and do not approach the actual conditions or our view in any way. Fundamentally, the Government drafts are nothing more or less than a codification of constitutional principles, legal regulations and administrative practice, all of which are the cause of the present state of affairs. We shall also be able to prove that the drafts pay special attention to the way in which the Czechs who have been moved to the German area since 1918 can be safeguarded, whereas the sense of a new arrangement is not the petrification of the injustice which has developed since 1918, but a guarantee of full equality—not only for all citizens, but also for all peoples and groups of peoples within the State.

" When the Premier, in the name of the Government, tries to prove that there is no purely German area, it is noticeable that he bases this on figures of the position caused by the State and State-assisted measures since 1918. The attitude of the Government is to ignore the demands of our draft of June 7th, and thus to refuse the establishment of national administration units based on the state of the population in 1918. They will never be able to make us accept the results of the Czechishization (*sic*) action in our German homeland.

" For the Government to demand the establishment of the national self-administration in the framework of the territorial self-administrative associations of heretofore means that our proposal of the sole practical and necessary form of real self-government is rejected.

" On the other hand, I assert that it is impossible to bridge the gap between the proposal of the Government and our proposal, since you start out with absolutely different and actually contradictory views. You regard the State as solely your State, which has to serve your needs first of all. You thus regard yourselves as the only nation entitled to lead the State. You grant the other nationalities and groups only a subordinate position with all its attendant results. You thus regard the Sudeten Germans merely as a minority, only give them special protective rights, and create for them extraordinary regulations.

" We, on the other hand, desire and demand a form of State which grants us no special protective or extraordinary rights, and which does not disqualify us as a minority. We want the German group to be the partner with full rights of the Czech people, and to have our people assured of the same political and legal position.

" Your view of the Czecho-Slovakian Republic as your national State has resulted up to the present day in the position that the non-Czech nationalities and groups could only have minority rights in all State institutions, and never equality, so that, for example, the non-Czech representatives in Parliament

APPENDIX

of the nationalities and groups are perpetually minorities, and thus helpless in view of the majority decisions of the Czech Parliament majority. That this is to remain so is emphasized by the statement of the Premier:

It is clear that Parliament, as the representative of the unitary State sovereignty, cannot be dissolved into partial organs of State, by which the activity of the central body would be restricted.

" Your proposal would maintain and strengthen your domination by means of majority decisions, even in the name of self-administration in the different areas. Your drafts, and the words of the Premier, show not the slightest sign of concessions in the direction of the sectioning of the State and central authorities, as proposed by us. The central system is, therefore, to be retained. In this way the democracy in this country remains a dictatorship of the constant national group which is numerically in the majority. We, on the other hand, must stand by our attitude which demands from the State that certain questions specially touching the vital interests of the different nationalities and groups should not be decided by the mechanical, purely arithmetical, and permanent Czech Parliament and Diet majorities alone.

" We do not go so far as to demand the dissolution of the central Parliament nor do we break up the main central authorities. But we demand the legal and technical measures which ensure the corresponding position of the different nationalities and groups in the central Parliament and in the central authoritative body. Your view of the State means that a Czech majority exists even in each self-governing province. The Czech national State views are, therefore to come into full play in the administration of the areas, so as to guarantee the unrestricted Czech domination in and of the units of the State. We shall prove that the national curiæ in the areas form no obstacle.

" According to the Sudeten German view of the State, a nationality State can only be practically and lastingly formed when real self-administration is introduced in its borders for the different nationalities and groups.

APPENDIX

" You see in the predominance of the Czechish people the being and vital law of the Czecho-Slovakian Republic.

" We regard such a state of affairs as unprincipled, impracticable, and as a constant danger to the peace of Central Europe.

" We wish for a common exercise of rule by practically regulated collaboration of the peoples and groups living in the Czecho-Slovakian Republic.

" You do not wish to take any cognizance of the nationalities and groups as such in a legal and other sense in the legal scheme.

" According to your views, the Czech language must be given absolute predominance.

" In our opinion, the equality of the languages of the nationalities and groups must be established."

Appendix B

THE census figures, to which I have already referred, cannot be taken as showing the true percentage of non-Czechs. If 3,400,000 people claimed Sudeten German nationality at a non-secret Czech census, we may be sure their numbers are really higher, but that the others, to prevent dismissal or other forms of persecution, preferred to call themselves Czechs. Seven hundred thousand said they were Hungarians. But who would be surprised if this number were much larger? Supposing a secret census, on the lines of a British election, were taken. What would happen?

One is entitled to assume that these official figures are not reliable. On the contrary, we can be almost sure that there are really about 800,000 Hungarians, 4,000,000 Sudeten Germans, 200,000 Poles, 2,700,000 Slovaks, 600,000 Ruthenians, and 30,000 Rumanians who have become citizens of the Czech Republic against their will. On this basis, which is certainly much nearer the truth than the other figures, we find that in reality the Czechs are a minority. The population is, therefore, made up roughly as follows :

Czechs	...	...	...	... 45.5%
Germans	...	...	...	... 25.0%
Slovaks	...	...	...	... 17.7%
Hungarians		...	...	... 5.3%
Ruthenians		...	...	... 3.3%
Poles	...	...	...	... 1.7%
Jews	...	...	...	... 1.5%

In other words, the Czechs themselves are also a minority, and there is no nationality which numbers 50% in all.

The following statistics, which are undisputed, show that I have good grounds for these assumptions.

APPENDIX

Between the years 1880 and 1910 the German population of the area now known as Czecho-Slovakia rose by about 565,000, i.e. by about 19.3%. In the same period, the Czech population rose by 1,200,000, or 24%. If the results of the first Czecho-Slovakian census of 1921 are compared with those of the Austrian census of 1910, a remarkable contrast will be seen between the German and Czech population curves. While the Czech population grew by 345,000 or 16.2%, the Germans fell by 519,000, or 14%.

Such a trend cannot be explained by any natural process. On the other hand, it is obviously the result of different statistic methods. The Austrian census was taken according to the mother tongue of the people; the Czech according to the nationality which the people acknowledged. This "acknowledgment," however, enabled the Czechs to make use of their political and social powers to influence members of the different nationalities. Promises and threats may well have persuaded many of the Sudeten Germans, Hungarians and Poles to "acknowledge themselves" as Czechs. I had a clear example of this recently in Prague, when a man who could not speak more than a dozen words of Czech told me that he "considered himself a Czech" since he was a Czecho-Slovakian citizen. His case was not a proof of pressure on the minorities, for he was a naturalized Czech subject. But he showed me his passport, and said he was proud to be a Czech. Czechs whom I questioned admitted they regarded such a man as a "Czecho-Slovakian," despite the fact that he knew no Czech. The Czechs are pleased to have anyone "acknowledge" themselves to be Czech.

This method of influencing the census figures was clearly possible, since, as already remarked, the census officials in numerous cases filled in the forms themselves. The census of 1930 was officially on the basis of the mother tongue of the people, but the principles of the previous census, the "acknowledgment" of nationality, were often applied. In cases of marriages between a Czech and a non-Czech the whole family was registered as Czech, for example. The establishment of Jews as a separate "nationality" in Czecho-Slovakia also led to a change. Every Jew, even though he had no knowledge of Hebrew or Yiddish, was registered separately, and the Hungarian minority claim they lost 65,000 of their votes in this manner. In mixed areas, the Jews thus have at times a key position, numerically speaking.

One especially noticeable happening was reported in the organ of the Czech Social Democratic Workers' Party, the *Pravo Lidu.* Two census officials had to be selected in a community with 578 non-Czech and two Czech inhabitants. The result was : two Czech census officials and 578 non-Czechs who were not selected for the post.

It is clear that the census figures are of the greatest importance, for upon them the size of the various nationalities is based. But the modern statistics do not look correct, even to the most casual observer.

For example, in 1880 there were 2,900,000 Germans in the area now Czecho-Slovakia, while in 1930 this figure had only risen to 3,200,000, or by about 10%. In the same period, the Czech population rose by 45%. It is natural enough for the population to grow, and if we compare the growth of the German population in other areas for the same period, we shall find it is immensely higher than 10%. In 1921, when the Slovaks had not as yet awakened to their fate, similar conditions prevailed between them and the Hungarians. The latter suddenly fell in number, while the Slovak population grew, as compared with 1910. Remarkably enough, the total Slovak and Hungarian population reached in 1921 just the same figure as in 1910.

One might argue that doctoring a few figures would make little difference, but this is an error. Precisely 20% of the population of an area must at least acknowledge one nationality in order to have the right to make use of their own language. Supposing in a given area that of 300,000 people there are 60,000 Sudetens. They may use their own language. It only requires one of them to be registered as a Czech, and the whole situation changes. Naturally, it often enough happens that there are 20.1%, 20.05%, or 19.9%, 19.85% or the like Germans or Hungarians, Poles or others in a district. The small fraction per cent. decides their fate. Registering (say) all who cannot read or write as Czech, since they could not understand what was being done in any case, would often turn a legal minority into a number below 20%. That is why I insist that only impartial foreigners should be in charge of a plebiscite. Whatever nationality in Czecho-Slovakia did it there would be no satisfaction. Even if the figures were correct, the " losing parties " would continue to believe they had been deceived. And one cannot deny that a census official would have the opportunity of falsification, which by no means implies that he would make use of it. As, however, mainly Czechs have been census officials up to now, the other nationalities would never agree to the results. I am convinced that the figures I have already quoted would be confirmed by such a plebiscite.

Appendix C

The Economic Fate of the Sudeten Germans in the Czecho-Slovak Republic

THE Sudeten Germans whose inclusion in the Reich was realized a few days ago were subjected during the last two decades to an economic pressure which undermined more and more the supports of their national existence and which threatened finally to lead to a steady decline of their racial power.

In the first place, the Sudeten-German territory was hard hit by the dissolution of the Austro-Hungarian Monarchy—just as was Austria, the present German Ostmark. Three-quarters to four-fifths of the total industry of the double monarchy was located within the borders of the newly-created state of Czecho-Slovakia, and of this share again 75–80% was located in the Sudeten-German border districts. However, by the drawing of the new borders, this industry's domestic market was reduced from 53 million to 14 million consumers, so that it had to seek a foreign market for the greatest part of its production. But in this it was confronted by the greatest difficulties, due to the fact that the industrialization of the other successor states and the promotion of agriculture in Czecho-Slovakia had to a great extent destroyed the former division of labour between the agricultural and industrial territories of the old double monarchy and also due to the fact that the Czecho-Slovakian foreign trade policy considered to only a small degree the needs of the Sudeten-German industry. For example, the Prague Government showed little interest in the possibility, provided for in the peace treaties of Trianon and St. Germain, of a closer customs union between Czecho-Slovakia, Hungary and Austria. Instead of cultivating good trade relations with the traditional sales territories of the Sudeten-German industry, i.e., the South-

Eastern European countries and Germany, the Czech leaders endeavoured to bind the country economically with those powers from whose hands they had received the gift of the new state. The slight success of this " western orientation " of Czech foreign trade naturally did not even begin to make up for the losses suffered by the Sudeten-German industry as the result of the coolness of trade relations with Germany and some of the successor states.

Moreover, the Czech domestic market policy was not suited to ease the Sudeten-German industry of the heavy burden of an industry with a big over-capacity and to promote its adjustment to the new conditions. On the contrary : The Czech economic policy was in relation to the great problems presented by the change in Central Europe and later by the world depression not only completely passive—following in this respect the example of France and of the former regime in Austria, where also a decisive work creation policy was taboo—but in addition the Czech government discriminated against the Sudeten-German industry in favour of the Czechs in almost all the important measures undertaken and thus clearly entered into the struggle of nationalities.[1] The decisive blow against the Sudeten-German industry was delivered soon after the war. By the prohibition (beginning of 1919) of transfer of bank notes and bank balances between Czecho-Slovakia and the other territories of the former double monarchy, the Sudeten-German industry was deprived, for example, of a great part of its liquid funds, and thus within a few months after the establishment of the new republic, was driven into the arms of the Czech banks which are said to have been informed of the coming measures and which had made, therefore, suitable dispositions. Furthermore, the refusal of the new state to pay for the war-time deliveries of the Sudeten-German industry to the imperial army weakened the capital strength of the Sudeten-German

---

[1] This is testified to by a personality of such high international standing as Lord Runciman who stated in his letter to the British Prime Minister dated September 21st, 1938 : " I have been left with the impression that Czecho-Slovak rule in the Sudeten areas for the last twenty years . . . has been marked by tactlessness, lack of understanding, petty intolerance and discrimination, to a point where the resentment of the German population was inevitably moving in the direction of revolt."

economy, even though it is impossible to determine what part of the estimated 4.5 billion gold kroner in unpaid war-time deliveries was owed to the German industry in Czecho-Slovakia. Along the same lines were the capital tax of 1919-1920 and the regulation of the war loan obligations of the state, both of which hit German property not only absolutely but also relatively harder than they hit Czech property. Of the some 8 billion kroner in war loans subscribed in the territory of Czecho-Slovakia, at least 6-7 billion kroner were held by Germans, i.e., far more than corresponded to the property relations of the German and Czech national groups. The obligation of the state resulting from the war loans was now—with the exception of certain small amounts—acknowledged only if 75% of the nominal amount was paid up in cash once more, and even then, the war loans held by " privileged " creditors (banks, churches, municipalities, orphan asylums, etc.) only bore 5% interest, while the loans of the " non-privileged " creditors bore but $3\frac{1}{2}$%.

The land reform, which was carried out by Czecho-Slovakia in the post-war years, was also accomplished at the cost of the German minority. Of the total of 1.8 million hectares which were expropriated from 1919 to 1936 (mostly against only slight compensation),[1] 750,000 hectares were located in the German border districts, 591,000 hectares in the Hungarian and Slovakian districts, 162,000 hectares in the Carpatho-Russian district and only 250,000 hectares in the Czech portion of the country. In relation to the property held, the German loss was probably even greater. Nevertheless, by far the greatest part of the expropriated land made available for settlement was, even in the pure German districts, turned over to Czech settlers, especially to the Legionnaires. In this way, the migration of Czechs to German language districts, so characteristic of the past 20 years, was helped immensely.

Other and later measures of Czech economic policy also resulted—whether purposely or not—in the decline of the German element in the economy of the new state or in an

---

[1] The act even provided that no compensation should be paid to " people who had committed grave offences against the Czecho-Slovak nation during the World War," and thus made it possible to expropriate citizens who had only been loyal to the former legitimate government.

apparent disadvantage to the Sudeten-German economy. The preference for consumption taxes in the Czech tax system naturally hit the Sudeten-German industry harder than the Czech industry, since in the German industrial sector, consumption goods industries predominate. Furthermore, the shifting of certain industries to the interior of the country for strategic reasons was also at the sole cost of the German border districts and, indeed, the Czechs did not hesitate, despite the depression, to confront the German industry for military reasons with the competition of a number of enterprises newly established in the heart of the country. However, the most outstanding discrimination was the disregarding of German industry in the granting of government orders, for which the government tried in recent years to create a legal basis by all sorts of petty regulations as to the racial composition not only of the workers but also of the officials of the companies qualified to bid for such orders. According to figures of E. Winkler, even after the " reform " 250 orders granted from January 1st, 1937, to January 20th, 1938, to companies in predominately German territory, were divided as follows : 69.2% went to Czech firms, 7.5% to mixed firms and only 23.3% to German firms.[1] For work on the fortifications which have been constructed in the German border districts in recent years, the government used almost solely Czech workers brought from the interior of the country.

A further means of such "administrative" discrimination against the German group was the disadvantage to which Germans were subjected in the setting of production quotas (especially for the very important sugar, spirit and margarine production). Last, but by no means least, there was the Czech banking policy, against which many complaints were made on the ground that it hindered granting of credit to German firms—unless by that means control of the firm concerned could be secured. The difference in the support given to German and Czech banks contributed especially to the fact

---

[1] Even a neutral witness like Lord Runciman stated in his above-mentioned letter : " . . . there is a very general belief that Czech firms were favoured as against German firms in the allocation of state contracts, and that the State provided work and relief for Czechs more readily than for Germans. I believe these complaints to be in the main justified."

that the Sudeten-German banking system declined more and more, thus forcing German industry to seek loans from and to become indebted to Czech banks, above all the Zivnostenská bank.

This all resulted in the fact that the Sudeten-German economy for the last two decades stood on the shadow side of the Czech business development. The Sudeten-German economy had far less part than the Czech economy in the upswing which started after the severe deflationary crisis in 1922-1923 and which culminated in 1929. On the other hand, the depression hit the German section of the country far harder than the Czech section and in the relatively weak recovery which has taken place since then, the Sudeten-German district has had but little share. In addition to the above-mentioned discrimination, this is due to the fact that the domestic (and foreign) armament requirements, which have played an important part in this recovery, have helped German industry but little, first because it produces mostly consumption goods and second because it was deliberately excluded from the armament business. On the other hand, the recovery of the Czech economy from the effects of the world depression lasted only a short time. In contrast to many other countries, revival in Czecho-Slovakia set in only after the first devaluation of the Kroner in 1934, while recovery in consumption did not begin until 1935. Then already in Autumn 1937 there was a setback which was far greater than that suffered by other European countries. This setback hit the Sudeten-German export industries especially hard. The political disturbances during the current year have naturally aggravated the situation and, just as the decline in world trade, have weakened especially the Sudeten-German economy.

Two results of the continual disadvantages to which the Sudeten-German economy has been subjected, can be especially clearly discerned.

First the former pure German industry in the Sudeten territory was made ripe for acquisition by Czech bank capital. This can be seen approximately from the fact that in 1919 Germans controlled about 80% of the industry in Czecho-Slovakia. In 1936, this had fallen to 40%, and to-day it is probably still lower.

NUMBER OF UNEMPLOYED[1]
IN GERMAN AND NON-GERMAN DISTRICTS
OF CZECHOSLOVAKIA
PER 1,000 INHABITANTS
End of August

I. CZECHOSLOVAKIA, TOTAL

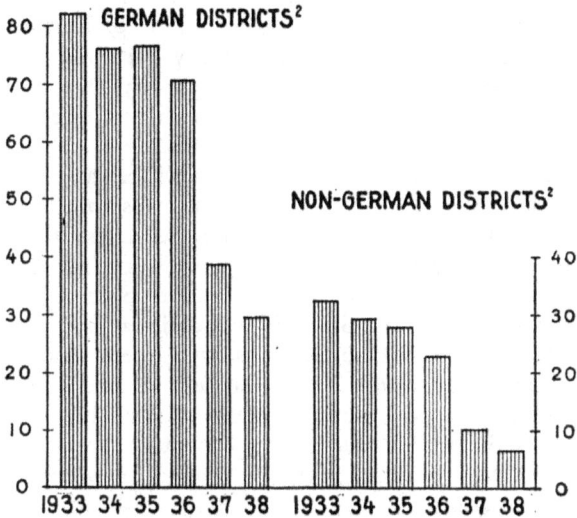

GERMAN DISTRICTS[2]

NON-GERMAN DISTRICTS[2]

1933 34 35 36 37 38   1933 34 35 36 37 38

II. BOHEMIA AND MORAVIA-SILESIA
INDUSTRIAL DISTRICTS   AGRICULTURAL DISTRICTS
with a German share in population of:

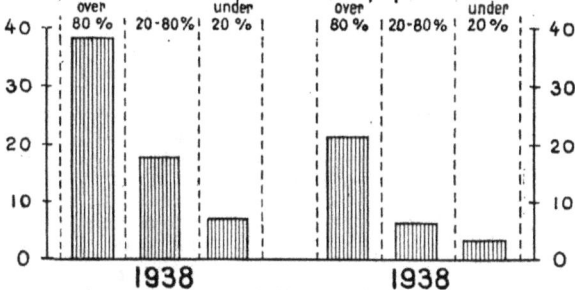

over 80% 20-80% under 20%   over 80% 20-80% under 20%

1938   1938

[1] *Persons seeking work, according to the figures of Ministry for Social Welfare*
[2] *Share of German population in total population greater resp. smaller than 50%*   I.f.K.38

APPENDIX

The unemployment figures are just as characteristic : Ever since it has been possible to compare unemployment in the German districts with unemployment in the non-German districts, that of the former has been many times greater than that of the latter. While, for example, in August of this year there were in the non-German districts of Czecho-Slovakia 6.5 unemployed per 1,000 inhabitants, there were in the predominately German districts 29.3 per 1,000. This proportion does not change if districts with approximately the same economic structure are compared. On August 31st, 1938, there were in the Sudeten-German industrial districts (where Germans make up over 80% of the population) 38.7 unemployed per 1,000 inhabitants, in the industrial districts with a German population of 20 to 80% the number of unemployed was 17.9 per 1,000, while the figure for industrial districts with less than 20% Germans was only 6.9 per 1,000. The figures for the agricultural districts were 20.8, 6.0, and 3.0 respectively. Thus, unemployment in Czecho-Slovakia was national fate, or, better said, German fate. Where Germans lived, there wandered the ghost of unemployment. Where the new masters of Bohemia and Moravia settled, unemployment was slight. Probably nowhere in the world was unemployment so great as in the Sudeten-German territory, formerly called the pearl of the Hapsburg kingdom.

Many have written in an affecting fashion of what this

European Countries with Highest Suicide Figures
Number of suicides per 1,000 inhabitants

	1932	1933	1934	1935	1936
Czecho-Slovakia					
Total	3.0	3.0	3.1	2.7	2.8
Sudeten-German districts	4.4	4.5	4.4	3.9	.
Austria	4.4	4.2	3.9	3.7	4.0
Hungary	3.5	3.2	3.3	3.1	.
Germany	2.9	2.9	2.9	2.8	.
Switzerland	2.7	2.6	2.6	2.6	2.8
France	2.1	2.0	.	.	.

economic distress has meant for the racial force of the Sudeten Germans.[1] The dwelling conditions were crying to heaven.

[1] See, for example, Kurt Vorbach ; " 200,000 Sudetendeutsche zu viel ! " München, 1936.

APPENDIX

The infant mortality was abnormally high for one of the most progressive districts of a modern industrial state, and the sickness records were horrifying. How this nibbled at the roots of the racial power of the people is realized when one learns that the Sudeten-German region reported the highest suicide figure in Europe and that the birth surplus of the Sudeten Germans decreased from year to year (just as in Austria) and

Natural Population Movement in Separate National Groups in Czecho-Slovakia and in Germany

Year	German	Czecho and Slovak	Hun-garian	Polish	Car-patho-Russian	German Reich
Live births per 1,000 inhabitants						
1930...........	18.4	22.4	28.3	39.5	42.9	17.6
1933...........	15.3	19.0	23.8	25.1	36.6	14.7
1934...........	14.9	18.4	22.9	23.7	35.9	18.0
1935...........	14.0	17.6	22.7	21.6	35.9	18.9
1936...........	13.7	17.2	21.6	19.8	34.6	19.0
Deaths per 1,000 inhabitants						
1930...........	13.7	13.8	16.4	19.1	20.0	11.0
1933...........	13.5	13.3	15.9	16.7	18.8	11.2
1934...........	12.8	12.9	15.1	16.4	17.9	10.9
1935...........	13.4	13.1	15.1	16.0	17.7	11.8
1936...........	13.0	13.0	14.7	15.0	19.4	11.8
Birth surplus per 1,000 inhabitants						
1930...........	4.7	8.6	11.9	20.4	22.9	6.6
1933...........	1.8	5.7	7.9	8.4	17.8	3.5
1934...........	2.1	5.5	7.8	7.3	18.0	7.1
1935...........	0.6	4.5	7.6	5.6	18.2	7.1
1936...........	0.7	4.2	6.9	4.8	15.2	7.2

threatened gradually to turn into a birth deficit, although unlike the Ostmark (former Austria) one-third of the population was not crowded within the bounds of a single city. Therefore, just as the Austrians seemed to be on the way to steady decline before the union with the Reich, the Sudeten Germans seemed near their death-bed, when they were saved by inclusion in the Reich.

Structure of the Sudeten-German Economy

The economic structure of the Sudeten-German region is determined mainly by the geographical elements of the German settlement districts in Bohemia and Moravia. The greatest part of the Sudeten region lies on the western, northern and eastern borders of Bohemia and Moravia and stretches from the mountains surrounding these two districts back into the Bohemian and Moravian plains. The German region consists mostly of mountainous and semi-mountainous country. As a result, it is rich in forests, but possesses only a moderate amount of good agricultural land. For this reason, the population of this region was forced early in its history to make up for the scantiness of its land by handicraft and industrial activity. Thus, German Bohemia is one of the oldest industrial regions in Europe. In the latter part of the Middle Ages, the Bohemian mountain region was a famous mining district, with silver as one of the main items of production. Later it became to an ever-increasing degree a centre of manufacturing, especially of textile manufacturing. In the former Austro-Hungarian monarchy, this region—after the elimination of the domestic customs restrictions—became the industrial centre of that tremendous economy. In the last 20 years, during which the Sudeten region has been part of Czecho-Slovakia, the structure of its economy seems to have changed but little, despite the almost continual economic depression.

The structure of the Sudeten-German region must of necessity be determined by arranging the occupational census of Czecho-Slovakia according to the various nationalities and by drawing from the figures for the German part conclusions concerning the Sudeten region. This method is relatively reliable, since the so-called " closed " German settlement district in Czecho-Slovakia (that is, the German settlement districts bordering on Germany) include about nine-tenths of the Germans living in Czecho-Slovakia and, furthermore, the borders between the Czech and German districts are quite sharply defined.

If the results of the occupational census for the German section of Czecho-Slovakia are compared with the results of the occupational census for the Czech section, a clear picture is given of the occupational classification of the Germans and Czechs in Bohemia, Moravia and Silesia since only a few Czechs and Germans live in Slovakia.

It is clear from the following table that the Sudeten-German region is more highly industrialized than the Czech section : not less than one-half of all Sudeten-Germans were engaged in industry and handicraft, while in the case of the Czechs the figure was about two-fifths. In the post-war years the share of those engaged in industry and handicraft has increased some-

what in both sections, and in both there has been a rather sharp
decrease in the share of those engaged in agriculture. However,
in absolute figures, the increase from 1921 to 1930 in the number
of Czechs engaged in industry and handicraft was three times
as great as the increase in the number of Germans engaged in
this field, despite the fact that the Czechs in Czecho-Slovakia
outnumbered the Germans only two to one. This means that
industrialization has made more progress in the Czech national

Occupational Classification of Germans and Czechs in Czecho-Slovakia[1]

Ocupational Group	Population according to 1930 census	Change 1930 compared with 1921		Per 100 inhabitants	
		absolute	%	1921	1930
Germans					
Agriculture, forestry, fishing	744,346	— 108,002	— 12.7	27.29	23.03
Industry and handicraft	1,469,756	+ 108,160	+ 7.9	43.59	45.48
Trade, banking, transportation	417,027	+ 34,327	+ 9.0	12.25	12.91
Public service, free professions, army ..	170,118	+ 518	+ 0.3	5.43	5.26
Household and personal services (other occupations)	430,441	+ 73,117	+ 20.5	11.44	13.32
Total	3,231,688	+ 108,120	+ 3.5	100.00	100.00
Czechs					
Agriculture, forestry, fishing	1,997,672	— 317,426	— 13.7	34.41	27.33
Industry and handicraft	2,882,363	+ 331,135	+ 13.0	37.92	39.44
Trade, banking, transportation	1,054,909	+ 295,948	+ 39.0	11.28	14.43
Public service, free professions, army ..	482,620	+ 87,081	+ 22.0	5.88	6.60
Household and personal services (other occupations)	891,336	+ 184,754	+ 26.1	10.51	12.20
Total	7,308,900	+ 581,492	+ 8.6	100.00	100.00

group than in the German national group. The development
in the fields of trade, banking, transportation, and public services,

[1] From E. Winkler: "Die Tschechoslowakei im Spiegel der Statistik," Karlsbad-Leipzig, 1937, page 69.

free professions, and army shows even greater differences. Here the absolute increase in the number of Czechs was some more than eight to almost twenty times as great as the increase in the number of Germans.

A comparison with Germany shows how highly industrialized the Sudeten region is :

Employment according to Important Economic Groups
in per cent. of total employment

	Census	Agriculture and forestry	Industry and mining	Trade and trans-portation
Germany	1933	28.8	40.6	18.4
Czecho-Slovakia	1930	38.3	37.4	12.2
Germans in Czecho-Slovakia	1930	23.0	45.4	12.9
Czechs in Czecho-Slovakia	1930	27.3	39.4	14.4

The Sudeten-German region is thus more highly industrialized than Germany ; in the whole world only two countries, Belgium and England, are more highly industrialized. In Belgium (1930) 48.9% of all gainfully employed were engaged in industry and handicraft while in England (1931) the figure was 49.9%. There is a striking similarity between the German region in Czecho-Slovakia and neighbouring Saxony where the natural and historical conditions of development are closely related to those in Sudetenland. In Saxony, too, the economic upswing began with mining and then turned to manufacturing, especially textile manufacturing. Moreover, the degree of industrialization in Saxony is quite a bit higher than the Reich average. But there was one fundamental difference between the economic development in Saxony and in the German section of Czecho-Slovakia : in the last decades the Saxon industry has been able to develop due to the size of German economy and in the last five years, due also to the national-socialist leadership, while the Sudeten-German industry did not have the advantage of a large domestic market and a sound governmental economic policy, and was hit hard by the political disturbances.

APPENDIX

The Sudeten-German Industry

In 1918, Czecho-Slovakia obtained the following percentages of Austria's industry[1] :

Industry	%	Industry	%
Sugar	92	Shoe	75
Glass	92	Leather	70
Jute	90	Paper	65
Glove	90	Metal	60
Malt	87	Beer	57
Textile	75	Foodstuffs	50
Chemical	75	Spirits	46

If the German element participated to an important degree in building up this industry under the Austro-Hungarian monarchy, it also kept an important place in the industrial work of the new Czecho-Slovakia, even under the difficult conditions during the post-war years. This was due to three factors :

1. Distribution of property-holdings.

2. Share of German-speaking workers, employees and entrepreneurs in total number of employed in Czecho-Slovakia.

3. Massing of industrial companies in the German language districts.

Distribution of Property Holdings

Information as to what firms in Czecho-Slovakia were or are controlled by Germans must necessarily be indefinite. For there are no official statistics on this subject ; and private investigation is often based on external factors which are not absolutely definite (capital participation, number of Germans on board of directors, type of administration, etc.). Nevertheless, it can be stated with a great degree of surety that a decade ago the textile industry, the porcelain and glass industry, the lignite coal industry and the musical instrument industry were largely controlled by Germans. The German element was also very strong in the paper industry, the electro-technical industry, the sugar industry, etc.

[1] Figures from Karl Janovsky: "Das industrielle Antlitz des Sudetendeutschtums in : Deutsche Zeitschrift fur Wirtschaftskunde," 1. Jahrgang, Heft 3. Leipzig, 1936, page 268.

APPENDIX

Of course, these figures are for 1927; in the meantime, the German property holdings have declined. Furthermore, by no means all of the firms under German administration or owned by Germans are located in what were the German language districts of Czecho-Slovakia.

Classification of Czecho-Slovakian Industry according to Ownership (around 1927).[1]

Industry	Number of Employed	Share of German firms in %
Mainly " German "		
Textile industry......................	245,000	89
Glass industry, including glass jewellery..	96,000	88
Porcelain industry	15,000	90
Lignite coal industry.................	41,000	80
Chemical industry...................	25,000	60
Musical instrument industry...........	6,000	90
Electro-technical industry.............	12,000	70
Mainly " Non-German "		
Aircraft industry	.	0
Armaments industry..................	.	5
Automobile industry..................	.	15
General engineering industry	.	18
Shoe industry.......................	.	15
Pharmaceutical industry	.	30
Match industry	.	30

The Share of Germans in Industrial Employed

The second factor—the size of the share of German-speaking employed in the total number of those employed in industry in Czecho-Slovakia—also points to the importance of the German elements in the industrial life of the country. The following are approximate relations between German and Czech property-holdings, according to the occupational and industrial census[2] of 1930:

The total number of those engaged in industry in Czecho-Slovakia was 5,147,000, of which 1,418,000 were Sudeten-Germans and 53,000 Carpatho-Germans. This is an average of

[1] From figures of the Czech economist G. Hejda. See Dieter Bleibtreu : "Besitzstand und Gefahrenlage des Sudetendeutschtums," Karlsbad, 1935.
[2] Calculated from figures given by Albin Oberschall, "Berufliche Gliederung und soziale Schichtung der Deutschen in der Tschechoslowakei," Teplitz-Schönau.

28.59% of all those engaged in industry. This is a higher percentage than would correspond to the " population percentage " (22.53%). The share of the Germans was especially high in the groups, given in the table below.

Here, too, it can be seen that the consumption goods industries have given employment to more Germans than any other industry. Roughly estimating, it can be said that in 1930, about one-third of those employed in the consumption goods industries in Czecho-Slovakia were Germans ; in other industrial branches the percentage was only about one-quarter. This basic characteristic is also to be seen in the third factor—the share of firms located in the German language districts.

Share of Germans in Certain Industries[1]
1930 ; in thousands

Industry	Number of those engaged in this industry in Czecho-Slovakia	Thereof German	Share of Germans
	in 1,000		%
Glass industry	122.2	64.9	53.1
Textile industry	526.5	273.4	51.9
Paper industry	69.1	31.6	45.7
Stone and Earth industry....	290.8	96.6	33.2
Power industry............	38.5	12.6	32.8
Chemical industry	69.3	22.5	32.4

Industry in the German Language Districts

The industrial capacity located in the German language areas can best be shown by taking only the Sudetenland, because here the Germans live for the most part in connected settlements. The best measure is, in addition to the number of employed, the amount of installed horsepower, because in this way it is possible to get somewhat of a picture of the capital intensity of the firms. According to the industrial census of 1930, there were employed in industry within the German language areas 724,900 persons or 32.2% of all those engaged in industry in Czecho-Slovakia. In the same year, installed horsepower amounted to 830,900 H.P. or 28% of the total installed horsepower in industry in Czecho-Slovakia.

[1] Measured by number of those engaged in respective industries.

The Importance of Industries in the Sudeten-German Language Area 1930

	Number of employed	Amount of installed H.P.	Share in Number of employed	Number of H.P.	Average of both Shares
	in Sudeten-German area in thousands		in Czechoslovakia %		
Mining	42.3	112.7	34.9	26.3	30.8
Stone and Earth ...	59.2	56.7	35.8	29.6	32.7
Glass	42.3	29.6	66.5	78.1	72.3
Metal and engineering	89.2	105.0	22.8	14.3	18.6
Chemical	12.2	35.6	30.0	43.0	36.5
Textile	191.6	219.4	53.2	51.7	52.5
Paper	18.8	70.3	47.3	59.2	53.3
Graphic	7.5	4.2	23.2	21.4	22.3
Leather	6.6	6.8	28.6	25.9	27.7
Wood............	50.7	66.1	29.1	30.4	29.8
Foodstuffs, beverages, etc.........	59.2	93.2	24.8	18.3	21.6
Clothing..........	62.9	4.2	22.1	12.4	17.3
Building and construction........	76.1	6.8	25.6	22.2	23.9
Power............	6.6	20.3	34.1	36.5	35.3
Total	724.9	830.9	32.2	28.0	30.4

The preceding table takes the employed and the horsepower figures together and gives a classification for the various branches.

The industries with the highest German share are : the glass industry, the paper industry, the textile industry and the stone and earth industry. Several small industries, which are not given separately in the table, such as the porcelain industry, the musical instrument industry and the toy industry, are also located for the most part in German areas. On the other hand, only a few firms in the graphic industry, the clothing industry and metal and engineering industry are located in the German areas.

Thus the Sudeten-German region along the Erz and Sudeten mountains is one of the most highly industrialized areas in Europe. Some districts (e.g., Asch, Grasslitz, Weipert, Rumburg, Warnsdorf, Reichenberg, Gablonz) report that up to 70% of their employed are engaged in industry.

There are no definite figures for the value of the production of the Sudeten-German industry. But it can be estimated that in and around the year 1930, almost as much was produced here as was produced by the Austrian industry (the number of employed was in 1930 only one-fifth less than in Austria). This means for the period around 1930 a gross production value of surely over 4 billion RM., or somewhat more than two-thirds the monthly value of German industrial production. Probably about two-thirds of this production consisted of consumption goods—textile production alone accounted for one-quarter of total industrial production in the Sudeten area. Thus, just as in the case of Austria, the inclusion of Sudetenland in the German Reich will mean mainly an increase in the field occupied by the consumption goods industries.

At present, production value in the Sudeten area is probably less than in 1930. This is due not only to low sales prices but also to the decrease in foreign trade which has hit the Sudeten-German industries very hard, as they are to a great extent dependent on exports. Moreover, Sudeten industry has also been effected by the endeavours of the Czech economic policy to strengthen the Czech-owned industries. This explains why a large part of Sudeten industry finds itself to-day in great difficulties.

The Economic Situation in Germany

A. Business Indicators

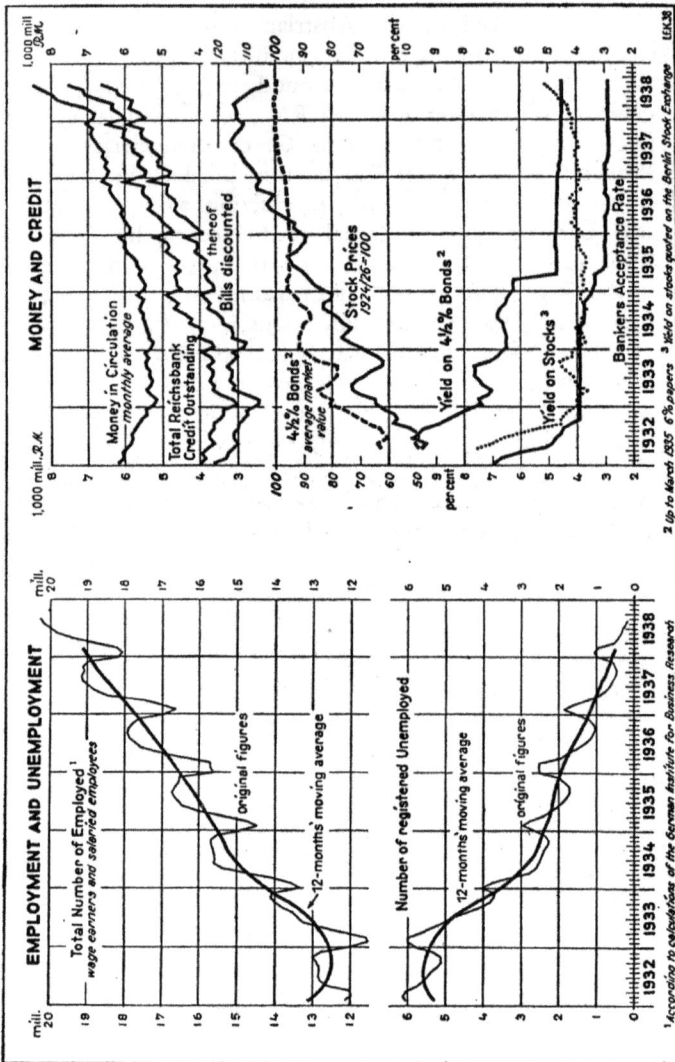

EMPLOYMENT AND UNEMPLOYMENT

Total Number of Employed [1]
wage earners and salaried employees

Original figures

12-months' moving average

Number of registered Unemployed

12-months' moving average

original figures

MONEY AND CREDIT

Money in Circulation
monthly average

Total Reichsbank
Credit Outstanding

thereof
Bills discounted

4½% Bonds [2]
average market
value

Stock Prices
1924/26=100

Yield on 4½% Bonds [2]

Yield on Stocks [3]

Bankers Acceptance Rate

[1] According to calculations of the German Institute for Business Research

[2] Up to March 1935 6% papers   [3] Yield on stocks quoted on the Berlin Stock Exchange

B. Statistics

Production, Employment Conditions and Wages, Domestic Trade and Consumption, Transportation and Communication

(For Statistics on Finance, Commodity Prices and Cost of Living, Foreign Trade see Weekly Report, September 22, 1938)

I. Production

Classification	Unit[1]	Monthly average				1937				1938							
		1929	1932	1936	1937	Sept.	Oct.	Nov.	Dec.	Jan.	Feb.	March	April	May	June	July	Aug.
Number of working days:						26	26	25	26	25	24	27	24	25	25	26	27
General Production																	
Gross value of industrial production[3]	billion RM; q. t.	21.21	9.45	16.34	18.15	.		19.07			18.35			19.05			.
Index number of industrial production (per working day)	1928=100; q. a.																
— including foodstuffs, tobacco and beverages — actual figures	m. a.	101.1	58.5	106.9	116.8			128.2		116.2	116.7			120.8			
— seasonal variations eliminated[2]	"	100.9	58.7	106.7	116.8			124.8		116.7	118.2			122.5			
— excluding foodstuffs, tobacco and beverages	"	101.4	54.0	107.8	118.8	124.9	125.6	127.2	121.7		121.0	124.6	125.6	128.8	126.9	129.2	
investment goods[3]	"	103.0	35.4	116.6	128.4	136.5	135.8	136.7	126.9		126.0	133.3	139.1	145.0	145.0	147.9	
consumption goods with elastic demand[4]	"	97.0	74.0	95.6	101.5	108.6	109.4	110.7	108.7	106.3	106.6	109.3	103.2	103.1	98.2	101.5	
World industrial production[5]	1928=100; "	107.6	74.3	117.8	126.2	128.0	125.1	119.3	114.3	113.4	114.1	114.9	113.2	113.3	113.4		
Germany's share	per cent.; q. a.	10.9	8.4	10.7	11.3			12.2			12.4			13.1			
Values of German industrial exports	1928=100; "	112.6	49.2	42.6	53.5			59.9			48.9			44.2			
Share of industrial production exported[6]	per cent.; "	23.7	24.9	11.4	13.0			13.9			11.7			10.2			

[1] t = metric ton ; q. t. = quarterly totals ; q. a. = quarterly average ; m. a. = monthly average. [2] Seasonal variations eliminated. [3] Investment goods are: iron, non-ferrous metals, machinery, building materials, trucks and automobiles, ship building. [4] Textiles, shoes, household goods and china, radio sets and toy. [5] Based on value. [6] Quarterly totals. [7] Since March 15, 1938, including Austria.

The Economic Situation in Germany (continued)

I. Production (continued)

Classification	Unit[1]	\ Monthly average 1929	1932	1936	1937	1937 Sept.	Oct.	Nov.	Dec.	1938 Jan.	Feb.	March	April	May	June	July	Aug.
Number of working days :						26	26	25	26	25	24	27	24	25	25	26	27
Production in Individual Industries (per working day)																	
Building Activity in Cities[2]																	
New building[3]	1928=100 m.t.	104.2	25.7	114.0	119.9	135.7	102.4	110.2	91.5	79.4	91.5	119.3	135.7	116.9	132.9	154.6	116.2
Building completed (inspected)[3]	,, m.a.	106.1	34.5	94.7	105.0	107.7	157.0	123.3	115.7	118.5	89.8	75.9	82.1	92.5	103.2	79.2	92.5
Pig iron[4],[5] & [7]	1,000 t	36.7	10.8	41.8	43.7	45.0	45.7	45.7	45.2	46.4	48.2	49.7	49.3	51.4	51.8	52.4	51.1
Steel ingots[4],[6] & [7]	,,	53.3	19.0	62.9	65.1	65.9	65.9	71.6	67.9	72.5	73.8	72.9	75.8	78.6	75.6	76.2	74.7
Rolling mill products[4],[7]	1,000 t	40.8	15.0	47.1	49.7	50.6	50.6	54.0	51.6	51.7	52.6	52.5	53.8	56.6	55.0	55.5	55.3
Anthracite	,,	539	344	520	605	601	620	640	625	638	632	618	604	611	595	606	588
Coke[4]	,,	105.6	52.3	98.9	119.5	121.2	122.6	123.7	124.2	124.5	125.9	125.5	124.2	125.7	126.2	126.5	128.5
Lignite (brown coal)	,,	572	400	530	605	615	633	657	656	658	630	602	611	628	621	635	617
Electric power prod. (122 plants)	1928=100	117.9	90.4	154.5	183.0	184.7	196.2	213.2	216.0	213.0	197.4	190.0	199.8	196.4	183.6	190.0	193.4
Gas[4]	1,000 t m.t.	105.8	93.2	101.4	110.8	113.0	113.1	117.5	123.9	121.9	122.3	118.0	114.3	114.4	112.9	49.9	45.0
Mineral oil	1,000 t	8.6	19.2	37.1	37.8	40.6	41.6	39.3	40.0	38.6	37.2	51.5	49.3	47.5	47.1	49.9	45.0
Chemicals	1928=100 m.a.	91.8	50.9	95.3	116.9	112.9	122.1	127.8	131.2	132.9	132.4	126.3	126.2	121.0	5.50	5.86	5.84
Potash, K₂O	1,000 t	4.85	2.54	4.70	5.51	5.50	5.92	6.44	6.19	6.76	7.09	6.87	5.96	5.86	5.50	5.86	5.84

II. Employment Conditions and Wages

Classification	Unit	1929	1932	1936	1937	Sept.	Oct.	Nov.	Dec.	Jan.	Feb.	March	April	May	June	July	Aug.
Employment and Unemployment																	
Total number of wage earners and salaried employees[9]	1,000 e.m.	17870	12580	17140	18870	19119	19141	18975	18120	18079	18228	18831	19401	19857	19993	20170	20270
Number of unemployed[10]	,,	1892	5575	1593	912	469	502	573	995	1052	946	508	423	338	292	218	179
Number of persons receiving benefits[11]	,,	1453	2536	923	538	242	257	301	578	738	650	300	237	183	153	115	88

[1] t = metric-ton; m. t. = monthly totals; m. a. = monthly average; e. m. = end of month; [2] Communities with over 50,000 population. [3] Public and industrial construction and residential building; [4] Per calendar day. [5] According to figures published by the " Wirtschaftsgruppe Eisen schaffende Industrie," [6] Including welded steel. [7] Since March 15, 1938, including Austria. [8] According to figures published by the " Wirtschaftsgruppe Eisen schaffende Industrie"; [9] semi-finished and finished products. [10] According to the calculations of the I. f. K. [11] Registered at employment offices; since March, 1935, including Saar District. [12] From the Reich Institute for Labour Adjustment and Unemployment Insurance.

Classification	Unit[1]		1929	1932	1936	1937	1937				1938							
			Monthly average				Sept.	Oct.	Nov.	Dec.	Jan.	Feb.	March	April	May	June	July	Aug.
Number of working days :							26	26	25	26	25	24	27	24	25	25	26	27

II. Employment Conditions and Wages *(continued)*

Classification	Unit[1]		1929	1932	1936	1937	Sept. 1937	Oct.	Nov.	Dec.	Jan. 1938	Feb.	March	April	May	June	July	Aug.
Employment in Industry (from industrial reports)[2]																		
Number of workers employed																		
All Industries	1936=100	m.a.	101.8	60.5	100.0	108.1	111.5	112.1	112.0	109.9	107.0	109.6	112.0	113.8	115.4	115.6	116.6	116.9
Production goods industries	,,	,,	95.7	48.8	100.0	108.7	113.5	113.8	113.5	110.2	106.2	109.8	113.5	115.9	118.0	118.7	120.3	120.7
Consumption goods industries	,,	,,	111.2	78.5	100.0	106.7	108.2	108.7	108.7	108.0	107.0	107.6	107.7	108.2	108.8	108.4	108.4	108.5
Number of salaried employees																		
All Industries	,,	,,	107.4	74.4	100.0	108.7	110.9	111.3	111.5	111.7	112.1	112.8	113.6	115.2	116.2	116.7	117.5	118.0
Production goods industries	,,	,,	102.7	64.8	100.0	112.0	115.1	115.7	116.0	116.4	117.1	118.2	119.4	121.2	122.6	123.5	124.8	125.7
Consumption goods industries	,,	,,	113.8	88.8	100.0	104.1	105.2	105.1	105.1	104.8	105.1	105.2	105.6	106.9	107.5	107.6	107.5	107.8
Average daily working hours[3]																		
All Industries	hours	d. a.	7.67	6.91	7.59	7.68	7.73	7.77	7.88	7.81	7.62	7.70	7.73	7.85	7.86	7.65	7.46	7.54
Production goods industries	,,	,,	7.72	6.86	7.77	7.87	7.90	7.94	8.05	7.97	7.76	7.82	7.87	8.03	8.06	7.99	7.89	7.91
Consumption goods industries	,,	,,	7.61	6.97	7.37	7.42	7.50	7.55	7.65	7.62	7.45	7.54	7.54	7.62	7.62	7.22	6.94	7.08
Number of hours actually worked																		
All Industries	1936=100	m.a.	103.6	54.8	100.0	110.2	114.4	115.5	117.2	114.3	108.7	111.8	114.7	118.1	119.8	117.3	115.6	116.8
Production goods industries	,,	,,	94.9	42.6	100.0	110.9	116.2	116.9	118.2	113.6	106.8	111.6	115.5	120.6	123.2	123.5	123.8	124.4
Consumption goods industries	,,	,,	117.0	74.7	100.0	108.3	111.5	113.0	114.7	113.7	110.2	111.9	112.2	113.7	114.0	107.3	102.8	105.3
			Yearly totals															
Income from Wages and Salaries[4]	billion RM	q. t.	44.47	26.00	35.86	*39.69*	.	.	*10·39*	.	.	*9.81*	.	.	.	.	.	.
			Monthly average															
Wages per Hour[5]																		
General average[6]	1928=100	b.m.	105.5	86.2	83.5	83.6	83.6	83.6	83.6	83.6	.	.	.	.	.	.	.	.
Skilled workers, male	Rpf	,,	101.1	81.6	78.3	78.5	78.5	78.5	78.5	78.5	.	.	.	.	.	.	.	.
Unskilled workers, male	,,	,,	79.4	64.4	62.2	62.3	62.3	62.3	62.3	62.3	.	.	.	.	.	.	.	.

[1] t = metric-ton ; m.a. = monthly average ; d.a. = daily average ; q.t. = quarterly totals ; b.m. = beginning of month. [2] All figures unadjusted for seasonal variations ; figures for the various branches and groups of industries are fully comparable only in their fluctuations, not in their absolute height. [3] Per wage earner : figures after point signify decimal parts of hour. [4] Gross income of workers, employees and officials (incl. Labour Service and Army ; excluding pensions). [5] Average tariff wage rate of the highest age group. [6] Average wage per hour for skilled, semi-skilled and unskilled male and female workers.

The Economic Situation in Germany (continued)

Classification	Unit	1929	1932	1936	1937	Sept.	Oct.	Nov.	Dec.	Jan.	Feb.	March	April	May	June	July	Aug.
		Monthly average				1937				1938							
Number of working days						26	26	25	26	25	24	27	24	25	25	26	27
III. Domestic Trade (Sales) and Consumption																	
Retail Trade																	
Retail Trade, total	1928=100 m.a.	100.4	62.6	76.5	83.5	79.5	88.9	84.4	133.6	73.7	76.1	83.6	92.8	85.9	82.1	84.8	·
Foodstuffs (incl. coffee etc.)	"	104.3	70.8	83.0	86.8	83.0	89.2	86.8	126.3	80.1	78.5	86.2	94.9	84.7	84.8	88.6	*89.0*
Textiles and clothing	"	97.2	57.7	73.2	83.1	71.6	93.2	83.4	156.7	71.4	81.2	84.1	95.4	92.5	81.4	83.2	·
Household furnishings	"	103.9	57.0	86.4	102.0	112.4	121.0	109.9	140.9	82.6	94.0	103.3	106.2	105.2	97.8	*102.2*	·
Consumption		Yearly totals															
Meat[2]	1,000 dz	33005	31725	34075	36366	2599	2778	3993	4742	3684	3388	3394	2791	2719	2505		
Sugar[3]	"	14930	13116	15110	16249	1253	1517	1629	1486	858	851	1144	1074	1269	1506	1697	1608
Foreign spices[4]	"	89.8	94.4	99.9	113.7	10.7	12.9	9.4	10.9	8.5	6.0	6.0	[12]5.7	4.5	5.3	4.1	6.1
Coffee[4]	"	1481.0	1296.9	1553.7	1778.5	142.0	141.4	153.2	170.1	150.3	153.1	145.1	[12]154.9	170.1	166.0	164.8	151.6
Tea[4]	"	57.6	47.9	45.0	49.8	3.7	4.3	5.1	4.3	4.6	4.1	3.6	[12]3.8	3.8	3.7	3.7	4.2
Cocoa, raw[4]	"	795.4	773.7	762.4	723.9	68.6	76.9	70.8	71.6	58.3	50.0	59.7	[12]57.9	68.1	39.5	54.9	51.0
Fruits, tropical and semi-trop.[4]	"	4963.8	5167.0	5827.4	3958.8	183.9	246.6	250.7	429.1	477.8	406.5	395.5	[12]288.1	338.0	309.1	240.4	816.6
Beer[5]	1,000 hl	56705	33345	39496	42677	3658	3360	2905	3420	3212	3008	3843	3513	3990	3915	3796	4247
Cigarettes[6]	millions	33285	31348	38217	41284	3719	3682	3420	3441								
Cigars[6]	"	6820	5495	8294	8736	749	746	820	774	699	694	802	679	745	711	711	748
Smoking tobacco[4][7]	1,000 dz	406.1	335.6	320.5	314.1	28.0	26.7	25.8	23.8	25.2	23.9	27.3	24.5	26.1	26.5	25.6	28.9
IV. Transportation and Communication																	
		Monthly average															
German Railway: Freight cars ordered per working day[8]	1,000 m.a.	152.1	99.8	135.2	146.7	153.1	161.9	164.7	148.7	134.2	140.3	147.7	149.4	152.6	151.6	153.9	152.1
Goods transported (Reichsbahn)[9]	1,000 t m.t.	36334	20170	33423	37305	39302	43223	43326	40210	34904	34015	40028	34046	38164	37259	*39844*	*41135*
River and canal traffic[10]	"			12719	14226	15601	16191	14809	14047	11262	13270	15100	13717	15345	15171	*16036*	*15171*
Shipping[11]																	
Arrivals	"		1513	2111	2389	2612	2561	2746	2597	2483	1988	2619	2654	2801	2834	3071	·
Departures	"		887	1249	1491	1652	1583	1574	1660	1448	1245	1319	1256	1173	1146	1230	·
Parcel Post (parcels handled)[11]	1928=100	95.5	78.1	102.4	106.2	102.5	110.3	120.4	151.2	93.4	103.1	107.4	115.4	112.5	100.5	95.7	96.5

[1] t = metric-ton; m.t. = monthly totals; m.a. = monthly average. [2] Animals slaughtered and import surplus. [3] Amount of sugar released for marketing. [4] Import surplus. [5] Amount released taxed and tax-free with export surplus subtracted. [6] Amount taxed. [7] Fine cut and pipe tobacco. [8] Excl. own use; incl. freight carried for national automobile highway construction project (Reichsautobahn). [9] Loadings and unloadings in the most important ports. [10] Incl. Rhine harbours since 1935 more expended figures. [11] Per working day. [12] Since April, 1938, excluding commodity trade of the Old Reich with Austria; therefore figures are not fully comparable.

For more books on this subject and many other little-known aspects of German history, please visit us at VersandbuchhandelScriptorium.com and our sister site wintersonnenwende.com !

Featured publications include:

• *Documents on the Expulsion of the Sudeten Germans: Survivors speak out.* Edited and with an introduction by Dr. Wilhelm Turnwald. Translated by Gerda Johannsen, Victor Diodon and Arnim Johannis. Translation in part © 2002-2021 by The Scriptorium and in part © 1951 by the Study Group for the Preservation of Sudeten German Interest, **as well as the German original:**
• *Dokumente zur Austreibung der Sudetendeutschen: Überlebende kommen zu Wort.* Selbstverlag der Arbeitsgemeinschaft zur Wahrung Sudetendeutscher Interessen, 1951.

• Kurt Vorbach: *200 000 Sudetendeutsche zuviel! Der tschechische Vernichtungskampf gegen 3,5 Millionen Sudetendeutsche und seine volkspolitischen Auswirkungen.* Deutscher Volksverlag GmbH München ©1936.

• Ingomar Pust: *Sudeten German Inferno: The hushed-up tragedy of the ethnic Germans in Czechoslovakia.* Scriptorium, Canada 2000-2022.

More titles are being added regularly in German and English.

www.ingramcontent.com/pod-product-compliance
Lightning Source LLC
Chambersburg PA
CBHW050743030426
42336CB00012B/1636